FIRE and RAIN

Selected Poems 1993-2007

Volume 1

RD Armstrong

Revised Edition

Lummox Press
PO Box 5301
San Pedro, CA 90733

Acknowledgments

The author gratefully thanks Tom Armstrong for his help in bringing this project
to fruition, Chris Yeseta for doing the layout and the editors of the following for
publishing some of the poems contained herein.

Books:
Unkissed By The Angels; And Love Is Dancing Just Out Of Reach; LAST CALL:
A Legacy of Madness; PEDRO BLUE; Mozart at 22; The Bukowski Page; Paper
Heart; In Memoriam; Fool's Paradise; Bone; Eyes Like Mingus; Maytag Heights;
Lost Highway; The San Pedro Poems; LUMMOX Journal; Last Call: the Legacy of
Charles Bukowski; The Hunger.

In the following magazines and anthologies:
Random Lengths; REPORT TO HELL #10 & 11; SHEILA-NA-GIG #10;
GENRE; Pearl 24; Chiron Review; Pearl 25; ON TARGET; Spillway; SIC; One
Dog Press; Black Cross; bender #1; California Poetry Calendar; Nerve Cowboy #
6; LUMMOX Journal; Wooden Head Review #8 & 10; Pitchfork; Vertigo Orb;
Haight Ashbury Lit. Journal #17; Raising The Roof (anth); Poet Noise; Sex In Public
#2; The Cherotic (R)evolutionary; Blue Collar Review; ZZZ ZYNE; CER*BER*US;
ArtLife Vol.19, #6; Lucid Moon; Unwound; Drinking With Bukowski (anth);
The Anthology of Orange County Poetry; Quercus Review; Louisiana Review;
Flash!Point; Bukowski Review; Poesy; Comme Ca Et Autrement; Gros Textes 30;
San Gabriel Valley Quarterly; Beyond the Pale #1; An Eye For an Eye (anth); So
Luminous the Wildflowers (anth); I Love Your Poetry; Long Beach Press Telegram;
Schuylkill Valley Journal of the Arts; St. Vitus Dance #2; Zen Baby; Cedar Hill
Magazine; Poultry; Meat; Black Ace #8; My Time – The Lunch Break Book (anth);
Telluride Watch; The Beatnik Cowboy #3; Poems-For-All #850.

In the following electronic magazines:
Black Cross E'zine; Yoni; Onedog Press; Zero City E'zine; The Open-ended It;
Spokenwar; Poetry Mining Co.; Poetry Webring Webzine; Thunder Sandwich; Poet-
rySuperHighway; Eroplay; Poets On the Line; Jazz Zine; The Ragged Edge; Author's
Den; Lazy Beat; Poetz; S.P.A.M.; Abalone Moon; Poetic Diversity; Poets Against
the War; DUFUS; Deliric; The Poets Encyclopedia; Moonday; Juice Online; M-
etropolis France; St. Vitus Dance; CP Journal #1.

PREAMBLE TO THE INTRODUCTION

When I came up with idea for this book, I was going to have it done by a different online printing service. Since then I've discovered another, much more flexible company. I decided to republish this edition, which was very uncharacteristic of me. I usually stay in the saddle of the horse I road in on. But it would be stupid of me to do that on this project.

So while I was republishing, I thought it might be right to reformat as well. So, this edition of Fire and Rain, Vol. 1 is going to be a bit different. I don't know if that will be good or bad...for all I know it might be bad form to do what I'm doing.

Too bad.

This is my book and I'm refining it to meet my desires.

INTRODUCTION

When I first started writing poetry, I had no idea that there was a vast community of poets who both wrote and read/performed their work to audiences of hungry listeners. Nor did I know where it would lead me. In fact, it wasn't until the early nineties that I even went to a poetry reading! But, once I did, I caught the bug (because basically, unlike most of my poetry heroes, I had a serious streak of "ham" in me). Actually, now that I think of it, I did go to a few readings before that, but these were "professional" readings with big name poets like Charles Bukowski. I never thought I'd become involved with anything close to that.

When I started writing poetry again in the early nineties, after a ten year hiatus, I discovered that my poetry had matured, as if that ten year period had allowed my words to season (just as I had seasoned). My poetry tastes had seasoned, as well. I think I had absorbed the 'body' of many of my poetry "heroes" – Bukowski being at the head of this list. I began to write prolifically (at least for me) and started to send out poems to the little magazines out there – 'there' being the crazy world of the small press. I had some luck, but I also had some hard times getting published. (After Bukowski it was nearly impossible in this 'rush to judgment' atmosphere of what was hip...it was a virtual vacuum of Bukowski-esque kitsch). It seems that, like life, there were always going to be those souls who think that they can make your poem better than it already is. Eventually, I grew tired of these games and decided I would do my own magazine (the Lummox Journal), where I could publish who, what and whenever I wanted. I figured I'd make some stamp money for my own submissions along the way and everyone would be happy.

There was just one drawback to this: doing the magazine and the other projects that sprang up from it (The Little Red Book Series, for one), left me with very little time to submit my own work to other mags and publishers. In fact, I had to publish my own books if I wanted any satisfaction. So, in trying to circumvent all the BS of submissions and rejections, not to mention the interminable waiting time-periods, I ended up providing others with the very service I was seeking.

This collection (volume's one and two) serves to present what I consider to be the best of my current catalog of poetry, representing a period of fifteen years (1993 to 2007). There are three exceptions, but because of the size of the three poems, I will be presenting them in a third volume entitled **On/Off the Beaten Path**.

As to the title, Fire and Rain seems fitting. Apart from the obvious connection to the James Taylor hit, this title resonates more closely with my experiences growing up in the 1960s followed by my resurrection as a writer in the 1990s.

RD Armstrong

TABLE OF CONTENTS

Steel 8
Vacancy..10
Spring Rose...11
Safe Sex..12
Real Weather..13
Pound Of Cure 14
Time..15
Pueblo De Las Putas 16
Nigger Bath 17
Midnight Blue 18
Pre-Performance Jitters...............................19
Blood Lines...20
For Chinaski 22
Graphic...24
Death Comes Stumbling 25
Dawn's Thin Red Line 26
Dark End Of The Street 27
Crazy 28
C.R.A.P...29
Corners De La Muerta..................................30
Class 31
Children Of A Loser God 32
Bullring 34
Box Of Rain...36
Box Of Joy..37
Angry Poets 38
And...39
Twenty Notes Gone South...............................40
Dreaming Of The Last Kiss 41
Johnny..42
Jesus Died 43
Instinct 44
Head 45
Hollywood Buddha......................................45
Hot Thoughts 46
Heat 48
The Gift Of Love For Kate.............................49
Nobody Knows More About The Future 50
Fat Man With A Stupid Grin............................51
Farther 52
Empty Moon, Foolish Heart.............................53
Denise 54
Old Cruel Town..55
Now As I Think Of You.................................58
Gaze..59
My Bed, My Rules 59
Night Falling Poets 60

Mozart At 22 62
A Moment Of Lucid Thought 64
On the Margin 65
Mina Lanza..66
Mauling The Innocence 67
Love Poem...70
Love, Pedro Style 71
Lost Soul 72
While Reading Lorca...................................73
The Lonesome Things 74
Livestock Of The Rich And Famous 76
Ritual 77
The Rescue Of Death 78
Red Petals..79
The Public Requires An Explanation 80
Rain In Venice 82
Punchline...83
Even A Piano Can Be Played With
  A Claw Hammer.......................................84
Paper Heart 85
Panhandler 86
Oven 87
The Pretty White Teeth Drip Death.....................88
One For The Old Man...................................90
Trained Monkey..91
Pinto 91
No Ready Made Hells 92
My Career As A Poet Is Dying Like
  Timothy Leary.......................................93
The Room At The End Of The Hall.......................96
T. A. B...98
The Queen Of Venice 99
The Old Dog...100
The Man Who Painted Birds.............................101
La Puerta Del Diablo..................................102
The Cheapness Of Life.................................103
Sunday Night After The Christmas
  Parade 104
Thanks For The Kiss...................................106
Street Opera 107
Stranger In The Bathroom 108
Speedball...109
A Winter Meditation...................................110
Yellow Man Sleeps 112
While You Were Out....................................113
We Are The Whirled....................................114
Esta Vida Loca..116

When The Last Tear Falls 118
Wall To Wall Emptiness 119
I Thought I Was 120
He Needed An Excuse 120
Goodbye Margaret Mead 121
Playing At The Edge Of The Grave 122
Work Gloves 124
Dish Water Anthology 125
Suddenly This Becomes A Task 126
Cry 126
Confirmation 127
The Vengeance 127
Bitter Pill 128
Bad News 129
6th & Mesa, Halloween 130
Travelin' Man 130
Crooked Smile 132
Aunt Rhoda's Last Request 132
Roller 133
Recipe For An Agonized Death 133
Raft Of Morphine 134
Yo Quiero 135
A Place In The World 136
The Peace Of Broken Glass 137
Something Overheard In A Dream 138
Other Women 139
One For The Poets 140
One Finger At A Time 141
Oasis 142
Nora Pushes Into America 143
Mangle Wine 144
Lost Highway 146
Maturity 148
Yvonne's Blue Shirt 149
Vacation 150
First Feelings Upon Reading A New
Book Of Poetry 151
Too Soon 152
The Stool 153
The Poem Will Save You 154
Karen 156
The Bastards Are Waiting 157
A Snapshot -1981 158
Sos 160
Turning In The Silence 161
Saturday Morning Driveby 162
The Moth 163

Mccoy Tyner At The Jazz
Bakery (10/02/98) 164
I'm Falling 165
I Look At Her 166
Horizon's Edge 167
His Brief Parade 168
Hate/ Love 169
Girl In A Red Dress 170
Four Short Poems 171
Eyes Like Mingus (For Steve Fowler) 172
I Must Be Getting Older 173
Another Day 173
A Tough Weekend 174
11:22 175
Growth Spurt 176
New Dawn 176
Without 177
Touch Me 178
Like The Wings Of The Butterfly 179
The Road (More Or Less Traveled) 180
The Rain 181
The Patient Bed 182
The Light Obscured 183
Tank Farm 184
Swallow 184
Table Scraps 185
Soutine's Palette 186
Saudade (For Monica) 187
San Pedro 188
Old Paint 190
Zoot 191
Love Ends At The Sidewalk 192
Group Therapy (Or One Man's
Tasty Morsel...) 193
Female Troubles 194
Graduation 196
Corazon 197
Coming Of Age 198
You Can't Car-Jack A Poem 199
Broken 200
When I Was 17 201
Lucid Thought #3 202
White Whine 204
Unseasonable Weather 205
Tweeker Afternoon 205
Tomb 206
The Shade-Tree Mechanic 207

FIRE and RAIN

Selected Poems 1993-2007

Volume 1

STEEL

I had been reading the letters of the "Old Poet"
and had gotten beyond
the mythological aspects
and beyond
the projection of
the presumption
that our lives of pain were similar
when
I came across the letter that summed it all up
for me.
The thing is like this:
you want to believe
that there is somewhere to get ahead to
but you have doubts.
Let's say that all the wrong turns
all the dead ends
all the unfinished ideas- turned to moldy lumps
all the unwritten inspirations
the unrecorded moments when the muse was speaking the same
language as you, to you
all the perfect little moments that
you failed to notice or appreciate
all those and then some will be/have been
lost underfoot as the mindless hoards march on
and you sit numbly
hoping that at the end of the trail
some sense will be made of all this.

The doubts congeal into fears while you are sitting
in a darkened room
daydreaming of a sexual encounter that will never come
or watching some kinda pornography
so you can get it up enough to get off
on fantasies so old and threadbare they are transparent.
Having the best sex in years
with yourself
cumming into a sheet and feeling that sad ecstasy-
knowing there's no one to share this aching with and wanting to
so badly
Wanting to stop being scared but not having the courage to act.
Dreaming of the taste of the gun barrel, knowing that taste
wanting to escape to something else, another life
and never having the courage to.....
Some of you will never fit
some of you will never survive the process of
fitting your round peg into a square hole
You will always be caught along the seams of the net
endlessly swirling at the edge of the
mainstream

or trapped like side-show freaks.
The factories will take their share
as will the "cool" mongers, the purveyors of "hip"
but some will survive
thru pathological perseverance
and others, like the Raindog, will struggle ahead
haunted by the stench of rot
the stale and musty smell of fear
mixed with the reek of decay
topped with a provocative sauce of angst and pathos
and sprinkled over with a little freshly grated death
just for that added spicy zip!

As each day progresses
as each hour unfolds
and each minute passes.
the glories and the gories continue
to floss the brain
in an eternal tug of war

I lick my lips and taste the steel, again.

VACANCY

There was no vacancy
in fact the whole place had been shut down
locked up
the contents of each room
covered with sheets
shades drawn
doors shut
locked
The paint is peeling
the foliage
dying
A fine layer of dust
covers
all.
I will clean the old place up
make it livable
again.
Slap some paint on
open the windows
unlock all the doors
air it out
Get out the "Murphy's"
clean, clean, and clean some more.
Clean and polish
the old sign
so you'll know
There's a vacancy
You're room is all ready
bed made up
flowers
fresh picked
on the nightstand
The register is open
and ready for you to sign in.
The staff
ready to serve you.
"Do you have any baggage?"

SPRING ROSE

I had this brief involvement
last spring
and here it is spring again
and I am thinking,
reminiscing really,
about the beauty.
The beauty of the moments
that pass between lovers....
The beauty of wildflowers
in a vase by the window
as lacy curtains breathe
and the light plays across the skin;
her skin,
your skin....

I am with you now
again in that room,
in that moment.

And just when I get to feeling
lonely for that memory,
that moment,
I also remember
the trip to the wildflowers
and the horrendous fight driving home;
screaming at the top of our lungs,
lane changes unnoticed
in the heat of battle;
this sobers my nostalgia....

Still, the vase and the curtains
breathing;
and the beauty of the moment.
The beauty of all the moments
strung together like beads
reminding one that it isn't all in vain....

And that if there is truly a balance
an equilibrium to this life,
then, perhaps, the moments will
eventually balance.

SAFE SEX

They come to my door
two or three times a week now
It's always the same
They always seem to know when
I'm eating dinner
They talk and talk and talk
about their lives
about their husbands
and boyfriends
They want someone to listen
to them
and I do listen.
And if there is any sex at all
it's always the "safe" variety:
They talk about it
and I listen
I try not to picture
the fingers groping
or the tongues darting
or the lips pressing
or the many and various ways
that one can fill the various orifices
with the bitter-sweet cocktail of "love".
Sometimes I get a hug
a reward for hearing their confessions
but mostly
they flit off into the night
back to their accursed husbands or boyfriends
or onto the next bizarre coupling.
And me?
I go back to my dinner
now cold and unappealing
much like my own sex life.

Real Weather

I thought of you today
and for the first time
there were no sadly played songs
in the background
No chorus of crooning caballeros
No chanteuse exhaling smoky lyrics
in a solo spotlight
I was not sitting at my usual table
in the corner by the bar
in the dimly lit twilight tavern
that sits at the bottom of heartbreak hill
on the wrong side of the tracks
in the bad part of
the town with no pity
that's located in the county strip
near the badlands
of my current
state of mind.

No, I sat by the window
Outside, the air charged with ions
the overcast sky, a sullen grey, threatened us with
Real weather.
And as I imagined the first raindrops
evaporating on the hot, dusty asphalt
the moisture absorbed into every tiny crevice,
I thought about you
You and your kindnesses sprinkled about.
At the end of a long drought
You were the first rain to blow across the fractured two-lane
that cleaves the God-forsaken little huddle of shacks
that I call home
mostly.

Faceless and Nameless you
You could piss on the empty, parched streets of my soul
and every molecule of nurturance would be
quickly and gratefully absorbed.

Now, like the street, I await the next sprinkling
from love's mystic fountain.

Pound of Cure

I thumbed through the phone book
found the number
and dialed;
RING
RING
RING
RING
"Can you hold?"
"Uh..."
"Thank you (click)."
Insultingly, friendly muzac began to play
in the earpiece of the phone
My head was swimming and I
was having a hard time staying focused
on the task at hand.
For some unknown reason
I was still on my feet,
still vaguely rational and
still hoping this was going to turn out okay.
I was coming to the end
of a year-long depression -enhanced
drunk.
I thought that I had hit rock-bottom
and if I couldn't get some help soon
REAL SOON
I'd wake up wearing nothing but a toe tag!
Then a very perky voice came
over the line:
"Suicide Hot Line! How may I serve you?"
"You're kidding?!"
"Oh no, sir! Suicide is a very serious problem
in today's modern world!"
"Say, do you mind if I ask you a question?"
"Why, no, sir; as long as it's not a personal one!"
"Where was your last job?"
"Pardon me?!"
"Where was your last job!?"
"I was the activities director at the Neuropsychiatric
Institute! Why?"
"Just curious, I guess."
"Excuse me, sir, but you don't sound very suicidal;
can't this wait until morning, say around nine a.m.?"
"Excuse me!?"
"Can't this wait, sir?"
I had to think
Could this wait until morning?
Could I delay my inevitable demise
for just a few more hours?
Through the drunken fog
a great flame of anger shot up

and in the darkest corner of my despair
an army of self-deluded thugs
began to sharpen their
tiny knives of deceit.
Oh, yes, there would be vindication!
Heads would roll
they would all be made to suffer
just as I had suffered!
"Sir? Are you still there?"
"Huh? Oh, yes, um, yeah sure, I can wait, uh huh....."
"Well, good! That's very reassuring! You have a good night!"
"Uh, yeah, you too."
I hung up the phone.
The room took a few more spins
and as the black tide came
swirling up around me
knocking me into the bar
I sank into the depths
and mercifully passed out.

I'll fix them
later

TIME

Something to do
while it's doing you.

Pueblo de las Putas

She stumbled down the sidewalk
fighting with a large white "sports" bag.
She wore a tight knit black dress
that seemed determined to ride up to an interesting height.
It was late, nearly one AM,
and I was heading south on Pacific
back to the point, back home.

I would've liked to stay and seen
who got the best of her first,
but the two gentlemen in the green
67' Chevy behind me had a different idea.

Later, back home, I remembered,
when I first moved to this town,
I thought that this was an awfully
friendly town.
The women on Pacific were always smiling
downtown
Smiling and waving
at me.

Then I began seeing some of them regularly
on the same street corners or hanging around
the same telephone late at night;
and I became suspicious.........

I was embarrassed by my lack of sophistication
and felt repulsed by these Putas
who had tricked me.

But then, one night, at a stop light, I happened to make eye
contact with one of these ladies
and in the blink of an eye, all the desperation, fear and anger
of all the long nights
strung out and lonely, the stinky sex on a dirty rag
hopelessly trapped hellish days
it was all there.

I saw the comedic twist amidst the ruins of her life –
waiting for a phone call to make her one fuck closer to that final fix.
And across town and several months later
a woman drunk on sex (or whatever)
stumbles home, her skirt heading North faster than she can.

Nigger Bath

"My daddy calls this nigger bath;"
she calmly tells me as she spritzes herself with perfume
to hide the stale odor of sweating through
another shift.

My heart aches at her vulgar racism
but I let it slide because she has something I want.

Hers is an inherent funkiness
an earthiness that reminds me of some of the women
I knew when I lived in the East Bay
in the early seventies.

She won't let "things" between us get out of hand
She's in control
I let her take advantage of me
I don't know what else to do.

We both know that this is just a moment in time
two strangers with excess baggage
My need to touch, to be touched
Her need to be touched.

I give her massage
she lets me
She gives me companionship
I let her.

We laugh at stupid, inane ideas
we come very close to being affectionate
But we are very mindful (she more than I)
not to get too lost in the mists of intimacy.

She thought that I might become her "in town man"
but that deal fell through.
When we first met, I thought she would be trouble
but, like Tom said, "I pulled on trouble's braids..."

Some day, she'll move uptown
or out west Texas way, to her rancherita
and I'll be here, still
like the air on this hot, June day.

We never kiss.

MIDNIGHT BLUE

A thick, moist blanket of fog
grey and fuzzy
was being pulled over
the foot of the peninsula
like a wool sock
He was driving south on Pacific
as little golden parasols
illuminated the street
and traffic whizzed by
He was driving slowly
in a big, Midnight Blue Lincoln
with a trunk big enough to
land on
I was trapped behind him
lumbering along in the '54
Just past the B of A he braked
swerving towards the curb
as if to park
"Good!" I thought.
But then at the last moment
here he comes
back into my lane again
"Damn!"
For two more blocks he does the
little dance
"Just who the hell does this guy think he is?"
Finally with a break in the traffic
I tug the '54 out and around him
and as I tumble past him
I glare down into the drivers seat
He was big
big and blue
with a dark sports windbreaker on
His hair was white and poking out
in all directions
like a bad "punk" hair-do
He held onto the wheel for dear life
There was an almost exquisite look of
agony on his face
Old Man Death was twisting
the knife into his guts and was
one twist away from canceling his ticket
I kept going
south up the hill
my way lit by the golden parasols
thinking about that horrible look
on his face

PRE-PERFORMANCE JITTERS

On the eve of my first reading
My hands sweat
And there's a conga line in my stomach.
But I'll do it
this reading
or be done by it
Stand or fall, on my own
without the aid of
my friend Johnny Walker
or any of his minions.

The solitary path sounds very appealing
but it wasn't my first choice
Sitting alone, hunched at a desk
dissecting 43 years of living
In a kind of do-it-yourself autopsy
Gleaning the verse from skeletal remains
or turning an insignificant moment into an allegory.
The current trend says
Poetry has to be performed
It has to be raised above the ordinary
that which we call "The life"
the extra-ordinary is that which we call "The art"
Both are, most likely, "the shit"
though in art, the shit is more cleverly packaged.
And into this minefield I come stumbling
with my little collection of verse
all set to amuse and amaze
Disgorging my soul
while my heart pounds on in fear
And why do something that scares
the livin' Be-Jesus outa me?
Why get outa bed ever again
Why bother to cross the threshold each day
I don't live (with)in fear
I live in spite of it.

BLOOD LINES

Families
I think about them
now and then.
I think about my own
My father
mother
sisters and
brother.
I grew up in the fifties
came of age in the sixties.
I came from a nice
middle-class
family
with nice
parents who
sent us to the nice public school system
where we were taught how to be good citizens
-Good Americans-
Selfless and hard-working
Long hours
Dedication
the whole "American Dream" plan.
I was raised to respect my elders
and not to judge people by their
"Race, Creed or Color"
but by their character.
Of course, I'd never seen a non-Caucasian person
prior to Junior Hi
Except on TV.
I played Little League for awhile
Wasn't very good
Showed artistic promise in school
Tended towards shyness
was kind of a loner
Still gravitate towards the edge of the crowd
when I don't know the crowd very well.
Wasn't a "bad" boy
Didn't run with a "crowd"
except towards the end of High School
and then it was the misfits club.
I survived the riots of '65
the assassinations of my heroes
the martyrdom of a generation
the last, lengthy military "police action"
the "Sexual Revolution"
the folk scene
I knew the words to all the Beach Boys songs
then I knew the words to all the songs on the first
Live album by Peter, Paul and Mary
The Beatles at Dodgers Stadium
Herb Alpert
Frank Zappa
Bob Dylan
I met Joan Baez once

Joni Mitchell was my oracle through troubled times
Simon and Garfunkle
were the bridge.

As I said
I grew up nice
but for some reason the niceties
have all but faded away
My nice parents
began to hate each other
(secretly, of course)
My nice family began to fall
apart
the nice schools became war zones
sometimes racial
sometimes ideological
Bob Dylan went electric
Hugh Masakela went into self-exile
Gandhi, who had died, hand outstretched to his assassin,
died anew with Dr. King
The open hand was filled with a weapon and "POWER"
became the watchword of the day.
Black Power, White Power, La Raza!
"Ask not what your country can do for you....etc."
begat "Hey, hey LBJ, how many boys did you kill today?"
which begat "There is a light at the end of the tunnel!"
which begat "Tune in, turn on, and drop out!"
which begat "The brown Acid is no good."
which begat "I am not a crook!"
My nice little world took a nose dive straight into the crapper.
The parents separated
then divorced.
I was expelled from home
like a Biafran refugee
forced to wander through the Gobi desert AKA the '70's.
My family went one direction
I went the other.
Now it's twenty-five years further on
down the road
I'm forty three going on forty four.
My family is scattered to the four winds
It is difficult to stay in touch
there seems to be no interest.
My brother and I talk on the phone three or four times a year
My mother lives five miles away, yet we hardly ever talk
I haven't spoken to either of my sisters
for at least three years.
Father and I rarely communicate at all.

Yeah, I think about families
sometimes
But it's best not to dwell on it too long
Better to sigh heavily
and hope for a better day
rather than be trapped
in the past.

FOR CHINASKI

I could never get it up for anyone like I did
for Chinaski
Oh, I tried the other boys (some of the old-schoolers were interesting)
but I didn't think the odds of survival in the nineties,
pretty boy, soundbyte, mini-mall, computer-enhanced,
MTV landscaped, SPOKEN word world,
would be too good, for the boys of yesteryear.
But Chinaski...
Now there was a man!
Chinaski was the voice, the Walter Winchell of the damaged, the drunken,
and the loner...
Chinaski took sloth and made it sound virtuous
he took debauchery and turned it into a democratic right
he made the D.T.'s sound like a rite of passage
and he cooed to us, he lulled us into bed
willing and able, wanting to be raped.
Chinaski
He worked the crowd like Elmer Gantry
he didn't have to pick your pocket while he mesmerized you with tales of ma
ness;
you paid willingly!
You bought that lake front property in Arizona-
you bought the myth...
Step right up!
Three for a dollar!
Chinaski was the whore with a heart of gold
He could blow away your troubles and mercifully let you sleep it off betweer
clean sheets...
Chinaski
Even the name sounded good, tough and clean
He was the "x" rated Indiana Jones, bullwhipping his way thru skid row
rescuing madwomen from nazi power junkies of corporate America
and their ass-licking toadies: "40 hour week" and "overtime".
He always kicked ass and even got some along the way, as he fought for the
next pint,
the next long shot winner...
Chinaski
he was the long shot that finally paid off
the horse that snuck out of the pack on the last turn
and beat the odds-on favorite by a nose.
And what a nose!
In his last days, as everything shrank, only the nose remained
feeding on the dying embers of his face, the nose loomed...
Chinaski
After cheating at so many things,
after cheating the hell outa life,

with only so many ways to cheat death,
only so many cards,
his hand played out, finally
Chinaski folded (someone else will cash in his chips...)

Chinaski

A name, a nose, a voice
Women
Hot Water Music
Ham On Rye
Post Office
Factotum
Love is a Dog from Hell
You get so Alone
War all the time
Mockingbird
The Days run Away
Earth Poems
Screams
Living on Luck
Betting on the Muse

The body of work lives on, the memory of the man lives on
But the body of Chinaski is gone,
vanished
And we...
We move on, excitement junkies waiting for the next turn-on
But I doubt I'll ever get it up again like I did for him
For Chinaski!

Graphic

She likes it graphic
this is what she says to me
She wants me to know that she
really enjoys a good
sweaty horse-fucking
with every nuance carefully detailed
She puts her hand on me
and tells me that she wants
a blowjob
but she settles for a shot instead
She goes home
her cunt on fire
to her man
I will go home to myself
but as I step outside
an old drunk carrying a bouquet of flowers
in a Taco Bell soda cup, 32 oz
molests me for spare change
and his girlfriend
an old, toothless crone
giggles as she staggers past and
I remember so many nights at the Redondo Lounge
drunken women giving me the eye
lipstick slightly smeared from too many
glasses of wine or vodka
Women old enough to know my grandmother
looking for someone to mother
or smother
then I think of my friend going home
horny and drunk
to her boyfriend
to fuck the living be-jesus out of him
or just to get sick and pass out on the bathroom floor
and I think to myself
"Things could be worse."

Death Comes Stumbling

Death comes stumbling through an open door
any door will do
Death isn't too choosey
these days
Death is overworked and underpaid
a day late and a dollar short
Death wants to take some time off
but is understaffed and can't get away
even for a coffee break.

I think about death differently
ever since that morning in January
when Death spun me around
and dropped me on the floor
like a rag doll,
my life flashing before my eyes,
the thread that tied me to this life,
unraveling while
you smiled
and nodded
at me.

Death isn't that melodramatic departure
that I dreamed of as a child
or that martyred sacrificial lamb
dropped in the service of some great calling
"Nobility of Sacrifice for the cause"
that I mistakenly longed for as a young adult
And, most likely, Death
will not come for me like an old friend
in my old age
to ease my ancient suffering.

Death will keep taking pot shots at me
like a weekend "plinker"
riddling that roadside sign until it drops
onto the shoulder of the highway
more air than sign.
Death will pick me off
like a scab,
one piece at a time.

DAWN'S THIN RED LINE

I look back upon a season spent in hell;
not the flaming screaming tortuous hell that
fires up youthful imaginations or terrifies
the righteous teetering on the brink of
judgment day 2000.
No the hell I speak of was tedious and solitary
with no thoughts of "kith and kin" except
long sad looks of *help me please*
that could not be comprehended.

It was a time in my life
that now seems almost mythic
dream-like, as if it never really happened to me
but was something that I read in passing
while standing in the checkout line
a story that briefly held my attention.
But it's all true
and I am reminded of that time again
for what reasons I can't imagine
except for a cold winter morning
crisp and damp in the storm's aftermath
and I recall the thin red line of a dawn years past
as if the mountains formed a rough-hewn dike
to stem the crimson tide.
Perhaps this memory is the vehicle for my thinking
I recall, about three years prior to that dawn, seeing
myself in the actions of some old
trashpicker, a scarecrow of a man
sorting bits of stuff into black plastic bags
bottles here, aluminum there, interesting items.
A human crow stockpiling his treasures:
bits of string and shiny baubles, bottle caps and plastic spoons.
And me thinking outloud
That could be me in a few years,
there but for fortune!
Not seeing that the joke would soon be on me.
Not fully appreciating the accuracy of my insight
until years later, when I recalled
my predictable (in hindsight) fall from grace
when I became that scarecrow
and spent my season in hell.

Dark End of the Street

dark cell
cold night
busy signal
no answer
dial a prayer
no answer
pizza boy
busy signal
suicide hotline
call back later
976-8bal
busy signal
pusher-man
no answer
desperation
walls closing
sharp inhale
phone rings
your boring life
a life raft
hurled into
stormy seas
I reach out
hang on
for dear
life.

CRAZY

The shoreline at the foot of the cliffs
calls me by my *real* name
my true name
calls me at night
late
when I am getting ready for bed
or sometimes
during broad daylight
when I am on a break
and distracted
not thinking
I hear the call.

It isn't a human voice
or the call of nature
no person speaks my name
Not even the voices in the walls
speak to me anymore
nor do the parking meters
or the alleyways.
Sometimes I hear my name
but no one is there
when I look.
No one is there
No one is there.

C.R.A.P.*

The smoothing out of wrinkles
might make a bed or your face look better
but it doesn't make for a better mousetrap
artistically speaking.
Nowadays
any fool with a paintbrush
is called genius
any clod with a piece of paper
becomes poet
any bozo with an amplifier
is a god!

Affirmative action might be good for business
but leveling the playing field
and organizing the players into teams
sanitizes the mystery and wonder
of this blood-sport
we call life.

The foundation of genius is built on crap
mountains of it
stables full
crap
being cranked out by every asshole
with a dream
We squat and squeeze
and out it comes
Behold! ART
It's controversial
It stinks
It draws flies
It is what's left over after
You extract the essence of life
and a lasting monument to our time
spent here
on this tiny rock
swirling into oblivion

Cut-rate Artistic Presence

CORNERS DE LA MUERTA

Sixth street
Ninth
First
Twenty second
Mesa and Tenth
Pacific and Thirteenth

Driving along Pacific
you encounter the
corners de la muerta.
A half dozen
shrines to the casualties
of blood alley
flowers and candles
wax and blood
sangria de los calles
Messages of hope and inspiration
hand-lettered on cardboard signs
praising the dead
bodies squished and mangled
by the very armor
that makes them
invulnerable.

Half the drivers on this
stretch
play a
hometown cross of
destruction derby and chicken.
Some drive without headlights
uninsured
a cold one nestled in their crotch
Other's
cars already wrecked
yet still able to move ahead
make mysterious lane changes
or surge ahead only to slow to a
crawl nervously watching for
flashing lights in the rear-view.
The muy boracho gently swerving
down side streets
going home or
to the liquor store
or the Laundromat
or just going
Este noche Death drives a late-model
sedan - negro y blanco -Quiet! Here he comes!

CLASS

"I know what makes a man happy!"
Oh yeah?
And what would that be?
"A man wants to be treated a certain way
He wants a whore in the bedroom
and a mother in the kitchen."
Marie says this to me with
that certainty that some children who
have been blessed by the wisdom of the ages
possess.
She says this to me as we lay on her bed.
It's the "odd" weekend and I have made the long
drive from Pedro to Montebello to try to
"fall in love" with her
yet one more time.
She says this to me and I know
she's serious, she means it
She doesn't understand that times have changed
Or maybe she doesn't believe me
As I tell her that
"I just want you to be a woman
wherever you are."
Marie was a firm believer in those mystic
feminine "guile's"
She used them on me constantly
unrelenting
"You're just denying your true nature as a man!"
She'd tell me
She would have me by the balls
and she would tell me that she knew me
better than I knew myself.
So, apparently she was also going to be my mother
in the bedroom, as well.
I finally gave up on ever falling in love with her
I already had one mother
(sometimes one is too many)
and I never did have much desire
for whores
but I wasn't a cheapskate either
I made sure that I left a good tip
on the dresser.

Children of a Loser God

Growing up to face the millennium
after being threatened with
the glories of impending doom
these children must now make a future
out of the moral rot and decay
that remains after a
decade and a half of
ETHICAL CLEANSING
conducted on behalf
(ours and theirs)
and with our silent blessing
by the major
economic powers.

The children of the
"LOVE" generation
of Hippies
Abbie Hoffman and Donovan
Janis and Jerry and Jim and Jimmie and Joan
under the protective wing of
Generation X(cess)
turning their faces towards
the hydrogen light bulb
praying for a death ray to
lobotomize them and
make them into
ZOMBIES!
TRULY,
FOREVER
AND
A DAY
These children of Generation
Why?
Me?
dead- 'Beats'
a contra- band
lovers of:
black leather, black hair, black lipstick, black finger-nail polish
black widow spider tattoos, black jackboots,
black "Goths" and "Vampires"
They're lost
futureless
disrespected
always hungry
never, ever fulfilled
never satisfied
You hear the agony

of their disappointment
in every word
see it in every look.
They could be models for
Rodin's The Burgers of Calais
or a Bosch interpretation of Dante's
Stages of Hell.

And Yet
by the light of day
they go to school
and work the nameless jobs
competing with the Mexicans
for the almighty dollar.
Still
they struggle ahead
smiling at dumb luck
and the sheer magnitude of
the days as
fate tosses the dice
Heroically battling the odds
these lost
milkcarton children.
Searching for a Never-Never Land
that no one thought
ever existed
Searching for a world
to get lost in
Looking for a way out
(but not forever)

These are
the Children
of a loser God.

BULLRING

"Hey man, nice pad!"
One of the literary stumblebums muttered
as he made his way past me.
It was cold and he thought
my pad would be warmer than
the meatlocker
it was.
"Got any smoke?"
The other one said as he stepped into the hallway.
He was graceful
like a matador
but it was a grace that could
set you up
for the sucker punch.
"Hey man, fix me up, okay?"
Sure thing, no problemo
I'm there for you pal,
buddy, amigo
Lots of snappy responses
danced through my head
all sounding like shit.
Instead, I nodded and headed for the kitchen
In my mind's eye the matador
flipped his cape over the bull's head. "OLE!"
"Yuh got any of that shit left?"
I dutifully got it ready
not even thinking about what I was doing
the subservient "good" wife
bowing her head
as the matador prepares to slip it in
up to the hilt.
I was awed by the hint of a nasty past
all I knew was
the matador had done time
When, how long, for what
It didn't matter
For all I knew
it coulda been for stickin'
his wife like a bull
and sendin' her ears to his girlfriend.

We huddled around the glowing pipe
passing the fire between us
I listened to them expounding
"So then Celine says....."
And they both laugh, knowingly
"Hey man, it's *war all the time*, you know what I mean?"
"Naw! You guy's live the shit! Me? I just write about it!"
"Don't kid me, you're right with us, in the trenches!"
"No, really, man, I mean, you know, I, um......"
The matador turns

and walks away from death
with dignity and style.
I
who never
fought
never picked a fight
refused to pack
heat
I
who's
library is
filled with poets
prissy and otherwise
books on ZEN
& Pacifism
& peace
I no
way deserved
the tough guy
sum bitch, mo fo, bastard!
reputation
that I've gained.
This literary stumblebum is the real deal!
I'm just a hack, Jack!
"Fuck man, what are yuh sayin'?
I try ta treat yuh like a friend
and yuh stab me when I turn
my back!"
The bull stumbles forward
confused
"Hell, I'll pay yuh!"
The matador unveils his sword
and the crowd goes nuts!
Despite my protests
they head out into the night
Adventure lays before them
and they will not submit
without a fight!

BOX OF RAIN

I am the earth
the soil
I am the rocks at the edge of the sea
I am hard because I have to be
because I have to weather this life
that rages against all of us
day in and day out
We are tough and hard because
this is a solitary life and there is no respite
certainly there is almost never any
comfort in this unrelenting drive
towards the end.

And yet
there have been times
when the tenderness of altruistic
compassion in deed or thought
has emerged from anonymity
to adjust my load
wipe my brow
or extend a helping hand.
It is a miracle of being touched.

I have been touched by this miracle
only a few times in my forty-five years
Yet each time I was infused with the strength
to continue my quest, renewed and cleansed.
And each time I remember this
I am able to draw from that memory
as if each touch was an ember that
glowed still, even in the darkest
corners of my past.

This morning, amidst screaming lovers
broken glass and the raging of hearts
as an ancient record pumped out its
own true wisdom
I remembered a distant morning
when I was touched by a friend's kindness
distracted, really, from the horrible
crunching jaws of life.
It was a simple gift: a paper with a word ritual
and a box of sand
and within the sand: a shell
some string and other things
Mundane items infused with meaning
becoming metaphors to guide me
through troubled waters and back home
to safe harbors...
"Look out any window, any morning, any evening, any day..."

BOX OF JOY

In my youth
when Bacchus was king
and the sensual
and sexual
were elevated to icons
to be worshipped
idolized
and mythologized
When "protection"
meant the prevention
of life
not death
When one's sexual identity
was not a social
faux paux
When I navigated
the waters
of the deepest ocean
Playing on the surface
parting the waves
with my bluntness
or plunging deep
into the dark
sounding
whale-like
only to resurface
jubilant and alive
thrusting and spurting
and gasping for air

In my youth
I could swim in this
fecund grotto
with far less repercussion
But now
as I wrap myself in the latex of nostalgia
I recall the many voyages of
my innocent youth
The beautiful sensations of
skin touching skin
of plunging into the depths
deeply
never wanting to come back
never wanting to think again
only wanting to part the waves
and plunge deeper than
ever before..

ANGRY POETS

Angry poets, like
Chollo Gangsta's cruisin'
low and mean
lookin' for any excuse
to go off on *anyone*
and beat them
into submission;
angry poets
lurking in the wings
cursing *everyone* else's
fifteen minutes
damning any
deviation from
the norm
as dictated by
the anger of their own
immediacy --
their own
self-involved
pathos
AS IF
they had a corner on
the market of pain
or anguish
AS IF
their wrongs could never
be righted
by the tender mercies of
time and forgetfulness
AS IF
they could steel their hearts
against the gentle
hand of forgiveness
and forever block
even the murmurings
of the little savage
beast that beats
within their rib cages.

Ease off, little one
ease off and let it go
even the black bird sings
a beautiful song

AND

The night is unfolding around me
and I am on the bridge
and the lights in the bay are calling
and the ripples make the lights dance
and I am pleased
on the bridge
as the night unfolds beneath me
and I speed towards Peedro
and the lights dance in the blackness
and I am pleased as I ride home
and life is finally making some sense
and I am pleased
and it is rare that I am pleased
satisfied
on the bridge
as the night unfolds inside me
as the big emptiness
opens its doors
and pulls me inside
and I remember that there's a big empty space
where you used to be
and I wish that I could fill that hole
tonight
as the night unfolds over me
and I lose your memory
again.

TWENTY NOTES GONE SOUTH

remember those beer-stained nights
of rompin', out-of-focus blues
when couples squeezed onto crowded dance floors
to dance the crazy-legged be-bop & jive, or
jumpin' at the woodside, or
doin' the crosstown, las' chance fo' romance-
closing-time boogie.
remember the band hittin' the ninth refrain runnin'
like a roundhouse haymaker findin' its mark
sweating under red and blue lights
while everyone was hypnotized by
the big man on the mic,
always dressed in a suit, Chicago-style
hair slicked back
remember how the big man never took off the shades
even at night, even as he slept, perhaps.
remember how he worked so hard
hunched over
cupping his instrument
pulling it into himself
grunting and shouting
sweat pouring off his brow
blowing his soul into and through
ten-holes
turning twenty notes into a
vocabulary of sighs and moans
like a mile-long, south-bound freight
pulling its tired load of joy and sorrow
over Breakheart Pass.
remember the big man driven
onwards
always

William Clarke is dead
twenty notes gone south, gone
home to rest

let us pause and remember

*In memory of Will Clarke, who died at age 45 on the road - early
November, 1996. A harmonica player and vocalist who specialized
in the blues. Rest easy.*

Dreaming of the last kiss

before the first kiss
has unfolded
I already know that what I want
ain't gonna happen
this time, 'cause
what I really want
is to press my soul into yours
two colors of clay kneaded together
two colors mixing into
something new
a different shade
another tone
a unique blend
one that neither of us
has ever had
before

And knowing that *that* is what I want
I wonder if you'll even
want me at all.

JOHNNY

Johnny
four days in country
bawling in pain
AK-47 shrapnel
ricocheting through his torso
like a steel ball
in a pachinko machine
Johnny
in a war that he
didn't understand
Johnny with his gun
ready to kick some Gook ass
instead
getting *his* ass
kicked.
Johnny
a regular at the V.A.
keeps the bits of shrapnel
they continue to remove
in a jar
with the lid screwed down
tight.
Sometimes at night
the shrapnel calls to him
pleading with him
to finish the job
that was started
years ago.
He sucks on the muzzle
of his pretty blue gun
driving his girlfriend
crazy.
He is disabled
and has learned to live in that system
has learned to live
with his disability
with his pain
with his slow death
by surrender
Johnny is already dead
laying down
waiting for some
words
and
a handful of
dirt.

JESUS DIED

I lay on the bed like Jesus
making a left hand turn
It's hot and dark
here in my cell
the fleas are moving slowly
creeping towards insanity
the sun cracks through
the seams of my ego
leaving me penniless
Jesus died jet black
and homeless
forsaken
his god no more apparent
than now

I lay on the bed
breathless in the dark
waiting
listening
passionless
in this brave new world.

Instinct

"Just what the hell is with you?
Don't you ever get enough?
Quit poking me with that thing!"
It's early
for us
only 9:30 in the morning
I'm laying beside her
in the morning warmth
the covers pulled up
to our noses
Her skin
lightly scented with almond oil
innocently calls to me
promising adventure
hinting at the pleasures that can be found
with the secret word
the right combination
that will unlock the door
The scent rises up to greet
the day
with arms spread wide
even though
she is
"Not a morning person!"
Her scent awakens me
and draws me to her
hungry
It pulls me towards her
exciting and stimulating me
beckoning me to enter her
promising delights
previously unknown
She's got the gun
but I've got the bullet!

"I can't help it, baby!"
It's like the salmon returning or
the humpbacks heading south
or that business with the swallows
They don't know why they do it either!
It's instinct!
Pure and simple
just
instinct

Head

Once I sucked the saline
opalescent
oyster juices
from the tiny folds and crevices
that lay beneath
Venus's glorious crown.

Now I survive on memories
and Hungry Man dinners.

Hollywood Buddha

I met the Buddha on the road the other day
we'd been playing phone tag
for weeks
I kept trying to make a date
but the Buddha is one busy guy
(as one would expect)
I met the Buddha on the road
and he asked me to help him
change a flat on his karma
later
we did lunch.

Hot Thoughts

"Today I could suck
the Folgers crystals
right out of the jar
and it wouldn't even
remind me of the cocaine
that messed me up
all those years ago."

"Maybe the earth is
wobbling on its axis
drawn into the sun
like a big blue moth
to the flame, making
it wander in its orbit
maybe that's why it's
so fucking hot, maybe."

"Satan has set up shop
across the street and
can be seen luring the
gullible and the young
into his parlor of dreams
enjoying this weather
he devilishly prods
recruits through the
blast-furnace door
using his big red tool
like a poker, much to
the delight of both
the boys and girls."

"The bartender talks of
Hitler as he cleans his
glasses, while the bar-
maids chatter excitedly
about the new shop up
the street, dreaming of
the mark of the beast
Satan's thumbprint on
their backsides so hot
it's so very, very cool."

"I dream of Eskimo women
chewing on my penis
then offering me an extra
serving of frozen eskimo
pie and upon digging in

a thousand Doves are joyfully
released and I am soon grateful."

"My world has become
a swirling fan, a shop
overwhelmed by the
white noise of metal
blades spinning, re-
distributing dead air
moving it about as if
it really mattered."

"Sitting in front of the
ice box with the door
opened, fanning my naked
skin, a cool wet towel
draped around my shoulders
I am slowly
melting into a puddle
forming at my feet."

HEAT

Mabel
Looked over at the young man
He must have been in his
mid-forties
A definite bohemian type:
old car
casual dress
Van Dyke
shades.
She wondered where he was going
what was he thinking
about
as they sat in the heat
of this summer afternoon
waiting for the light to change.
She wondered
what would it be like
to feel forty years of life
between her legs
again
muscles tightening
fingers gripping
her pillowy ass
"mules" delicately teetering
over her head
as he poured it into her.
Mabel
lowered her gaze
looking at Claude.
Claude
drooling
smiled weakly
and winked at her.
Forty-five years of marriage and he still had
what it takes!

The Gift of Love   *for kate*

I had hoped that the holidays
would pass through
like a weak
low pressure ridge
unnoticed.
Instead
a slow moving cold front
settled in
like that unwanted friend
passed out and snoring
on the couch
and threatened to make this
another reminder
of just how far out of the loop
I've slipped.

Except for one thing.

The gift of love
which was delivered to
the doorstep of my soul
by special messenger.
The gift of love:
sought for so long
by so many
for so few.
The gift of love:
from which a single strand
can sustain a heart
for years.
The gift of love:
easing the burden of
this life
lifting the load
just enough to wipe your brow
and soothe the troubled
and befuddled heart.

When you brush my cheek with your lips
and guide cupid's arrow into
your waiting heart
I know
(tho I can't believe it quite)
that the gift of love
will be here
for me
for many days to come.

Nobody knows more about the future, the past, the secrets of living right, the lost philosophies of health and happiness, and the answers to just about everything, than drunks and persons age 15 to 25

I was sitting in a bar the other night
watching my back
when a drunken woman
with sad eyes accosted me
She wanted to know if I liked her
enough to take her home
I declined
she sat down
and talked about
redemption
forgiveness
and jesus
christ I thought
will this never end?
Later on, her boyfriend,
a plumber by trade
an alcoholic by profession,
joined her
and I
and then *he* talked
about his family
and
forgiveness
and jesus
christ I thought
this *will* never end!
And then salvation
arrived in the form of
a yellow cab.

Fat Man with a Stupid Grin

Next to a picture of Meher Baba
sits one of you
looking up at the camera
from your perch on the couch.
shorts
No shirt
with your legs crossed.
Fat and sassy
not a care in the world.
Not the famous author
Bukowski, just
another old guy
enjoying the day.

A moment
captured
forever.

FARTHER

My father
even the word seems foreign
father
farther would be more honest
more real

My farther and I live our days
separate and distinct
We never brawl or throw fists
our arguments are always
very dignified
very correct

We have exchanged
polite
watered-down notes
sent them over
the great distance
that now separates
us
Two men
urbane
and reserved
lost to each other
out of touch
farther away than mere miles

Empty Moon, Foolish heart

La Luna
calls to me
arms outstretched
flowing hair
sprinkled with stars
flirting with me
She calls me by my secret name
"te amo, esse,
venga aqui"

Moon
as an empty plate
waiting for the second helping

Moon
as the light at the end
of the tunnel
guiding us
influencing our
emotional tides
as we ebb and flow
undulating through space
on this little
blue rock

Moon riding across
the black velvet, two lane
of a night sky like a
bored-out
flathead Indian
with the high beam on
crossing the double, yellow line
of the Milky Way
as it races against
time and tide

Moon
as a big zero
a big nothing
with nothing better to do
drawing me close
and whispering into my foolish heart
"Te amo, esse"
knowing your absence
has left me weak
and vulnerable
La Luna drives me crazy
toys with my heart
and will drop me like
yesterdays news
when she tires of me
just like you did.

DENISE

She dances naked except for a red blanket
which she holds in her arms
like a partner
She Tangos around the room
her left arm, high
her right hand, low
flipping the red hem
back and forth
much the way
flamenco dancers
flirt with the crowd
showing an ankle
a calf
maybe even a thigh
she is showing me
more.

Her pale skin
like butter melting
muscles rippling
beneath
the red blanket
a flag draped limply
on a windless day
the air in her studio apartment
too dense to breath deeply
a shape of sunlight
creeps up my leg
warming as it progresses
as I lay on her bed
at one with this day
at peace with the world
at least for a while
at least till this dance
is over.

OLD CRUEL TOWN

Long before the Hillside Strangler
twisted up inside with hatred
and began to disembowel
young "actresses"
in the back of a van parked
high in the Hollywood Hills
Or a model with a name
that sounded like ice cream
was snuffed in the high desert
above the Angeles Crest
and dumped in a hollow grave
off of Route 2
I took a job near the heart
of Tinsel Town.
I wanted to be a "filmmaker"
so a friend got me a job
with an independent film company.
The company had a 'studio'
conveniently located in the back of a
film lab just down the hill
from the intersection of
Hollywood Blvd. and
Western Ave.
right smack in the middle
of the red light district of
East Hollywood
where you couldn't walk ten
feet without running into
a porno shop
a porno theater
or a brothel.
This was the intersection of the damned!
Unbeknownst to me
my mentors haunted these sad
brick tombs
after dark after we'd gone back to our
respective domiciles
Buk and Waits inched along those grimy walls
out for a pack of smokes
a bottle
and maybe a little action!
By day the streets were filled with all manner
of strange creatures of varying
sexual preferences and tastes.
The hot breath of free "love"
and *enterprise*
mixed with the hot wind
that blew in from the desert
making everyone
more than a little edgy.
It was the Spring of 1974

Nixon was still clean
Washington was still the home of
truth
justice
and the American way
and I was making soft-core porn
for about a dollar twenty five an hour.
Any doubts that I had were allayed
by the slogan which was repeated
mantra-like by the other
"film students"
IT'S ALL IN THE NAME OF _ART_!

And so, in the name of art
we watched as sex was faked for hours on end
sweating under the lamps
with actors named Biff and Tawny
listening to a litany of moans and groans
powdering naked skin by the yard
and re-shooting from every angle
then known to man.

In the name of art
we made this crap:
" 4 Dames, 4 Dreams"
" A Day in the Cuntry"
" 3 Days to Live"
"Black Belt Brothers"
Also some scenes that were later
edited out of "Dark Star"
were shot after hours.
It was bullshit
all of it
the stain of bullshit touched
every facet
every person
every thing was a lie!
but that's the magic!
You turn SHIT into shinola
and convince the world
to buy it!
Eat it up, my children,
it's sooo good for you!
Don't worry about what it tastes like.
What? It tastes rancid?
You ignorant fool, that's the taste of DANGER!
That's the taste of LIFE, baby!
Wipe your chin....

So, in the name of art
we labored 'round the clock
shooting imaginary scenes
in the most makeshift

of sets
whilst outside
on the Avenue of Stars
out of work "actresses"
turned to their other 'trade'
trolling the Blvd of Broken Dreams
for producers
out-of-towners
businessmen and members of the
armed forces.
A blow-job took the place
of a resume
a calling card
a note from home.
More has been accomplished in the name of art by ass-kissers and cock-suckers
than all the "methods" combined!

Long before the veneer was stripped away
and Washington began to peddle
the new morality
(Doled out by the elected whores)
to the faithful
before the streets were overrun with
rough trade
and the concrete was contaminated by the perpetual
rain of diseased body juices
we stood and waited at the roach coach
ankle-deep in puss and blood
while the bosses of corruption and greed
was serviced by grateful
young actresses and actors
smiling and speaking their lines so convincingly
like debutantes
like royalty
never letting on how much their knees and asses hurt
as their "auditions" dribbled down their throats and thighs.

I never made the cut.
I stepped out of line
never reaching the doorway
which led to the glamour
and the fame.
I walked away
another loser
going south
on Western.

Now as I think of You

It's not the moments
where the knife is in your gut
or the nausea you feel
as the floor drops out below you
and you know it's over
or the smell of something
hitting the fan
or the sound of the
other shoe
hitting
the floor

It's not the smile
that fades away
or the stale taste
that replaces
the sweet kisses
or the softness of the touch
that becomes
course and
abrasive

It's not even
the tenderness
evaporating from
the words
these eyes
or this heart
that bothers me the most

It's this numbness
that I carry inside me
like a dead fetus

I dread
this whitewash that covers
all the moments
of everything
and leaves me with
this blank *nothing*
emptiness

I lean against empty walls
and there is *nothing* on my mind

GAZE

She pierces me with her stare:
two perfect
puddles of ink
I imagine I look like a deer
caught in the headlights
of a late-model destiny
Go on, then
hit me

MY BED, MY RULES

Perhaps I should have laid down some ground rules
when I let you lay down beside me
But I was so grateful
that you even
smiled
at me
that I let
you cross my
threshold no questions
asked
I wanted you to take me
and you did
hook
line
and
sinker

NIGHT FALLING POETS

My companion and I were
enjoying the night air
recently in a back
alley of San Pedro
it was filled with the
smells of Jasmine
Bar-B-Q sauce
and human beings.

and:
"Oh naked orb, thou
smiling visage doth kiss
my...iiiiiiiiiiooooooooooohhhhhhhhhh"
THUD!

GEEZUS! DID YOU HEAR THAT?
My companion squeeled.
Hear what? I replied.
THAT, THAT THUD AND
THOSE, THOSE WORDS, And all?!
Huh? Naw, listen, you need
to relax   unwind

and again:
"I'm silky smooth for you
baby, slide your azure blue
into my...iiiiiiiiiiioooohhhhhhhhhhhhhhhh"
THUD!

MY GOD! What was that?
my companion cried.
Oh that?
I replied
Oh That was nothing!
Don't even worry about it.

finally:
"I have seen the best
minds of my...iiiiiiiiiiiooooooohhhhhhhooooohhhhhh"
THUD!
"OOOWWWWW!"
There's someone out there!
My companion cried
leaping up.
Look! There's someone
laying on the ground
and AND There's two guys
bending over the one on the
ground!
Now, they're picking him up

and carrying him away!
WHAT THE HELL'S GOING ON HERE!
Don't worry, it's nothing, I tell her
It's like this everytime
the moon's full
The poet's bloom and then they
drop
It's nothing really
just be careful where you
step when you leave.

But what are those men doing
with the bodies?
They're homeless. They sell
the bodies for money
or they eat them

BUT THAT'S HORRIBLE!
Not really,
think about it
Poetry is feeding men's souls
so why shouldn't poets feed men's bellies?

Life feeds off art, once again

Mozart at 22

"My life sucks, man!"
He was 22
His hair was cut like the Dutch Boy
and dyed jet black
His overcoat covered
ragged jeans and jackboots
Leaning against the lamppost
bumming cigarettes from
passersby
A group of young men milled around him
muttering their agreement with
his wisdom and profound insight
he was 22 and life was
passing him by
He looked dejectedly at me
"Why can't I be like you, man?"
22 and he wanted to double his grief
In parts of Eastern Europe
old men of 22 were manning the barricades
right now even as we stood on a corner
in the midday sun
Mozart at 22
had already lived two thirds of his life
Rimbaud at 22 had given up poetry,
been shot by his ex-lover
and taken up gun-running
(better profit to cheap-thrill ratio, I guess)
"My whole life is totally fucked up, man!"
He lived in a small, neat, studio apartment just
down the street
When I was 22
I lived in a roach infested hole of an apartment
in Oakland
My girlfriend was two-timing me with
a baseball player
and booking herself on an all-expenses paid trip
around the bend
The Blue Meanies were gassing kids on Telegraph Ave.
whilst Nixon and Company
were looting Vietnam
raping our faith in authority
and pillaging the federal government

Now this kid
this 22 year-old
this angst-ridden lost soul
wants to be like me
living the "easy" life?
One tenth of my entire life

equals his "adult" l fe
His life is a little fa t
compared to the brown
crusty foot-long floater of a turd
that is mine
22 years old
and its all over except for the
screaming and cryi g
"Rest easy kid, it's always darkest
right before it goes
completely black."

A Moment of Lucid Thought

My friend writes of the incredible stupidity

of the universe
                        and I laugh in agreement
knowing that I don't really know
the full breadth or depth
of his statement
knowing that when my time
comes, for real (and not just in test-form)
I will be neither ready
nor laughing.

Most likely I'll go insane
while trying to open a pack of gum
in the parking lot of the 99 cent store.

On The Margin

A loose mirror on the passenger side
A leaky seal
King-pins that need replacing
A failing wheel cylinder
A broken camera lens
Bad tubes
Dull blades
Unpaid debts
Broken dreams
No hot water in the bathroom
Stains on the sheets
Dirty smudges on the walls
A weed choked garden
A hair-choked drain
A few steps from insanity
A few more steps from a cardboard box under a bridge
One step from an early grave
A strange hand in your pocket
A finger on the trigger
A pain in the ass
Blood in the toilet
A bald tire – a wet, oily street
The wrong time to turn over a new leaf
A broken rubber
A broken heart
An insensitive remark
A caution thrown to the wind
 Boredom
Four walls closing in fast

It's not the big issues that take you out
It's the little moments that ambush you –
A broken pencil
Or your computer crashing with all your poetry
Erased

MINA LANZA

She was tiny
maybe five feet tall
maybe
but she had a good heart
a big one
as big as the sky above the mesas.

I met her only once
on a cold night
many years ago.
I had just driven in
from Los Angeles
returning seven or eight
Hopi elders
to their homeland
near four corners
in the shadow of Black Mesa.

As I stood in her kitchen
shivering in front of the old
cast iron stove
the roar of the road still ringing
in my ears
She brought me hot cocoa
and blankets so I could
sleep on the sofa.

I remember little of our conversation
except that she was very kind
to me
a stranger in a strange land
a young hippy boy
who had driven close to
fifteen hundred miles to help
strangers.

It hadn't seemed so remarkable
back then
but now, as I recall
the hands of Mina Lanza
weathered and old
placing that glorious cup of hot cocoa
into my hands
sore from gripping the wheel
and the way she smiled
as she cupped my hands
with hers
I believe now that I was in the
house of an angel

MAULING THE INNOCENCE

Crystal blue sky
so blue it pierces the retinas
painfully
so blue it is indescribable
like the first drag
or the first high
the best blue that has ever been
sparkling
radiant
holy

A crystal blue sky
unfaltering
never fading
meets the brown loam of freshly churned earth
the blue belly of the sky
pressing deeply into light brown hills

The invisible accent of light
translucent and shimmering
highlights the crests of broken furrows
touches upon exposed boulder
and accentuates a sea of weathered stumps
They stand in mute testimony
dying but not yet dead
sap gurgling out of the heart rings
motionless
desperately rooted to this spot
the boneyard of a great forest
An entire ecology
a sanctuary of the living
it's once colorful palette multi-hued and brilliant
now nearly wiped clean
now reduced to the barest of hues

The wind that once ruffled leaves and feathers
that once wafted the piney scent
gently
now blows cold and unrelenting
not as funeral dirge but low and mean
like the cracked and creased faces under hard hats
that unleashed the fury on this place
The wind moans as it bends low
and works its way through the corpses
as if searching for lost kin
but finding no identifiable relic
in the carnage

A roar ascends the hills echoing
followed by a second

as two grimy yellow tractors lurch forward
These massive tools lunge into the edge
of once wooded glory tearing the smaller stumps
from the ground
prepping for the next assault
the final
necrophilial
raping

At the foot of the hill
two behemoths wait as men with hard faces
inspect their machinery
They are the scalpels and must be prepared for
this monstrous surgery
this hideous "facelift"
A chain of steel is attached between the
twin icons of American engineering
it's links as big around as the biceps
that heft the ends onto the waiting hitches
On every tenth link
a spike of steel has been welded
it's tip sharpened to a deadly point
forming a chain-saw to be dragged up this hill
behind these D-9's

A thunderous roar heralds the final act
as these knights in yellow armor march upwards
the line of brown and blue
their target
Plumes of smoke belch from their mounts
as they chug and labor onward
inexorably
like the crushing millstone of time
The thin chain
a wicked thread
trails behind forming a Cheshire grin
a crescent shaped scythe
mauling the innocence with idiotic perfection
Stumps are ripped out of the ground
their roots dredged up by this dragline
this horde of steel fanged mongols
and sent toppling down
like decapitated medusas
they litter the shredded dirt
or
some snag in the chain
roots and links entwining
temporarily forming
bizarre charms on this horrifying
charm bracelet

The air fills with the disharmonious chorus

of diesel engines revving
their powerful treads throttled ahead in bursts
gripping and grabbing the rubble strewn earth
sinking into the loam
catching and rumbling ahead
dragging the chain and it's harvest
onward
The chain
raking upwards
raises neither dust nor cry
It is lifeless
born in fire Phoenix-like
the dull scraping of stones as it clinks along
is buried in the din of cracking wood--
some stumps giving up their grip on stone and soil
with a loud 30-06 report
that even through the roar causes the cat-jockeys to flinch
and duck for cover
Or the air is sliced by an eerie cry
halfway between the shriek-like whine of
metal compromising metal
and the heart wrenching throatiness
of a melancholy cello
it's melody coaxed forth by the coarse caresses
of this hideous bow

It is a sound that plunges straight into the soul
piercing and burning like crystal blue ice
It is a sound that lingers in the air
even as the final aria is delivered from
the ramparts of uprooted stumps
It is a sound that will not blow away
that hovers still
even as the last notes of this earth opera
fade over the acme
It is a sound that will haunt the backroads of memory
until the silence of death

LOVE POEM

Lying beside you
in the darkness
listening to Joni Mitchell
on this hot July night
our arms entwine
your hair is in my mouth
my belly presses against your back
and
we breath softly
and slowly
and
I never thought
that I would
know
this
peace
again

LOVE, PEDRO STYLE

I've always had luck with the ladies
mostly bad
So it wasn't any surprise when
you came a rollin' & a tumblin'
into my life
You with your hand tooled holster
and your chromed hog leg
You were just some stale acid
that I found in a drawer
-long on promise
and short on delivery-
You were just a parking garage
that I got lost in
-You always said
you were number one-
You were just the next
nail in my coffin
-not the first and not the last-
You came and went
like a two hundred dollar
paycheck on a three hundred
dollar repossession Friday
I was just a comfort station on
your way to Easy Street
back to the land of milk & honey
where you could walk the streets
and be worshipped
by men and women alike
But do not be concerned about me
I'm gonna be just fine
You were just the boom
that I forgot to duck under
Just the other shoe dropping
Just the shit hittin' the fan
Nothin' much at all...

LOST SOUL

A Mexican on a bike
is trying to proposition
the crazy girl
as she cowers in the corner
of the bus stop at Fourth
and Pacific

She walks with a limp
and one hand is not much good
just kinda hangs there
as if she had a stroke
or some type of palsy
She's certainly been damaged
by some facet of life

I've seen her before
around town
Once I saw her hitching
in front of my house
with two boxes of laundry soap
She was not doing too well

I would have given her a ride but
I'd heard that she was a hooker
of sorts
from some friends
and I just didn't want to
be so closely involved
in her life

Her hair is sometimes
really messed up as if something
had been sprayed on it
and left to dry
I pause to consider the dangers
but the thought of yielding
to my carnal desires
is easily tempered by imagining
her drooling mouth
poised over me and
me grabbing a handful of
dark hair
matted and crusty
This never fails

The Mexican gives up and rides away
The crazy girl extends her hand
thumb up
into traffic
as the light changes
I put the '54 in gear and lumber forward
into the wilderness

While Reading Lorca

Always I am thinking of you
even at the oddest times
alone in the house
washing dishes
or taking a leak
while reading a book
or watching the news
or watching the gutters
turn red
first with rust
and then with blood
while reading Lorca
or Yeats
or Bukowski
listening to the blues or
listening to my friends
bantering
or conversations overheard
at a bar
or a cafe
you are just around the corner
rushing into
and through my life
on your way to somewhere else.

The Lonesome Things

Four in the morning
and I am awakened by the
staccato dripping of water
not from the tap
but rather
from the eaves
above my bedroom

Poking my head out the door
expecting a thick blanket
of fog
I find only the coolness of the night
with stars that twinkle
and shine
in the hugeness of the black sky

Laying in bed
unable to sleep
being pierced to the bone
by a long
and low
mournfully sad
fog horn
blowing its warning
to passing ships

My mind searches in vain
for a place to hide
a hole to crawl into
to escape from the sound
of this woeful sadness

Once years ago
I was awakened in the wee hours
by a sound such as this
but it was created not by a machine
but by a woman several blocks away
grieving for her animal
killed on the coast highway

As I remember this
I am chilled as another long
low blast penetrates me
like a steel spike
gently but with purpose

My mind jumps from point to point
as if browsing for some mantra
to focus upon
to lull it/me to sleep

but the horn
will not relent
the horn blows its own "judgment day"
dirge
and I cannot sleep

I think of all the lonesome things:
the lonesome shriek of a train whistle
the grieving moans of the widow
a chorus of dogs
moaning in pool hall harmony
to the sound of a distant siren
the lone wolf howling on a distant ridge
the moan and banshee shriek
of a ship as it runs aground
the death rattle as life moves out of your lips
the howling as the dogs pick up the scent
the sorrowful song of the loon or
the Winter-like dirge of Humpback whales
piercing the eternal black night
of deep waters
the eternal black night of
the soul
eternally
alone
alone in the dark
at four a.m.

LIVESTOCK OF THE RICH AND FAMOUS

She was hot
moving across the floor
like a cat
sultry and proud
under the thumb of no one
owing allegiance to no one
save her family.
She cut a swath
through the lives
of the young men
who swirled endlessly
around her
in a flurry of misdirected
passion.
She was Carmen
she was Media
Her acid tongue
dusted the cheek of many
a would-be lover
like the bull whip's kiss.
She flicked off the ashes
of their foiled romance
as casually
as she adjusted their libidos.
If you had a bulge in your pants
it had better be shaped like
a wallet.
She was Isadora
dancing before them
eyes twinkling
wantonly dipping low
reveling in her sensuality
flitting sprightly
teasing.
She was Lorena*
drawn to manly brutality
exasperated when she could not
tame it
and exonerated when she cut it loose.

*Bobbitt

RITUAL

Each day
each act
each breath
is
an expression
of this wondrous
creation

Each moment
savored
or
forgotten
is
a talisman
in the ritual
in this unnamable
pageant
this unfathomable
stew
in which life is only
part of the ingredients

Like a Turtle carrying
the world on it's
back
Or a lizard with
a map of the galaxy
on it's belly
Or the face of the Virgin
mysteriously
appearing on
a tortilla
We are touched
by the magic
randomly
or so it seems
even though there is
magic afoot
everywhere!

The Rescue of Death

Nadine Lockwood was four years old
when the relief finally reached
the side of her crib
It was a long road
When relief came for Nadine
as it has come for so many in this century of plenty
it was not the loving hand of mother
guiding her back to health
nor was it the graceful hands of intervention and kindness
It was, instead
the grim reaper gently guiding
Nadine down the hall and out into
the streets of shame
and, mercifully away from a world
where mothers and fathers
and sisters and brothers
do evil on themselves in the name of
"*GIMMIE!*"

Nadine Lockwood starved to death
One of seven children, she did not enjoy
the privileges of the Seventh Son
Her mother, who could only love six
little mouths, six little hearts,
her mother chose Nadine and marked her
for a death by isolation and neglect
Her mother, acting as an agent for
a world overwhelmed with children,
decided to thin the population
by *ONE* lousy little mouth
Who knows if Nadine would have amounted to much?
Who knows if she would have been
anything more than a burden
in a world already overburdened with
the malnourished and feeble-minded
offspring of parents, who
themselves, are numbed by
Poverty's incestuous relationship
with a greedy world.

Nadine is gone now
the memory of her will fade, with time
Not because we are insensitive, but
because time strips away *all* our memories
Soon we'll be awed by sexual harassment lawsuits
against six year olds and 'drug-dealing' teens handing out Midol...
And for Nadine Lockwood, who's death
is celebrated, quite unintentionally,
by the medium that hungers for and feeds off
the good, the bad and the ugliest
of this century of plenty,
the question "how could this happen?"
will remain unanswered.

Red Petals

Like the curved blade
of a Samurai
I dream of pushing
my sword deep
into love's scabbard
while scented petals
delicate and yielding
quiver
and drop
to the ground.

The moon is reflected
in the black water
of the well
its face is half-obscured
by the fallen blossoms of
yesterday's beauty.

The garden path
washed by my tears
will soon be
covered with
a blanket of red and
yellow.

The day does not
come easily.

THE PUBLIC REQUIRES AN EXPLANATION

I had sent some poems
into the mag
hoping they would publish
one or two
Rejecting me
I was informed that
one of my poems
(one of my favorites
as it turns out)
nearly made it
The woman informed me
that I could read at the
next open mic reading
for their next issue
and she hinted that this might
improve my chances
for publication
So I went to this reading
(which I thought went really badly)
and I read my poem
and some other poems
and I made some remark
about a bribe or something
not being big enough
So, later
I'm sitting next to her
and I jokingly ask if the reading
made a difference?
She looked me in the eyes
and said, very seriously
"Oh yes; now I know what you were *feeling*
about those whores."
I looked at her for a long moment
studying her face
her hair
her thinness
her perfectly round breasts
through the cleavage
of her shirt
I thought, briefly
what it would be like
to go down on her
Would she require an explanation
a description of my activities
in order to know
my feelings?
in order to have the appropriate
feelings in response?
Would she be less aware
would she feel less

if it was only a one way
experience?
Or would she be able to figure out
what was going on by
listening
watching
smelling
tasting
would she?
So, now I'm debating
sending in some more
The mag once was a forum
for unpublished
and unknown poets and writers
but now
with fame and fortune
it was becoming the MTV
of poetry mags
If you are a known commodity
if you have a "name"
then your chances are much better
It would be a lot easier
if I could just give someone
head
or take it up the ass
while I recited my favorite poems
about love
sex
death
and poetry mags

Rain in Venice

Raindrops
glimpsed through a doorway
as they land on a wooden deck
like fat bugs colliding with
a windshield.

The afternoon light
creeping yellow
across aged flooring
touches
the dirty edge
of the knife
that has just fallen.

Lightning bounces
off clouds
suspended horizontally
by unseen threads
Denise laughs
and claps her hands
excitedly.

PUNCHLINE

He sits amid a pile of debris,
the remains of past glories
and wild shopping sprees at
K-mart and Tar-jay,
while she paces nervously
around him, in need of a fix
They could be anyone:
a couple at the market
or drinking a beer in the cool of the evening
or just hangin' out with friends in the park
He sits dejectedly on a low step,
smoking and talking dramatically
as if someone cares or is listening:
"I swear to God, there was a time
when, maybe twelve years back,
we were the most envied couple
around. And now we've come to this,
this ending."
He gestures like an outcast king
I think of Nyugen Van Thiu, once
the guardian of South Vietnam
and now the proud owner of a
Liquor Store somewhere in Orange County
"Why, it's enough to make you think that
there is no God at all; that this has been
a joke
and not even a funny joke, but
one long, cruel joke!"
Grand words for no one to hear.
A garbage truck rolls up and begins to
load their possessions into the back
They stare at each other
a sad horror washing over their faces
blurring their features
then he stands, lights a cigarette, takes a drag
and gallantly hands it to her
They don't utter a word when the Garbage men
pick them up and toss them into
that great, dirty orange, gaping maw
And they hardly make a sound
when the jaws close over them

I don't get the punch line at all

Even a Piano Can Be Played with a Claw Hammer

Schubert wrote sad ballads
Ellington swung
Jerry Lee Lewis got closer
to what John Cage
had in mind
Satie played it one note at a time
While Zappa drew from Varesse
who played as many notes as he could
at any given moment
Bukowski played like a drummer
and Waits claimed it was drunk

You can pluck it like a harp
or tickle it like a foot
or coax the notes out
like the three little pigs
You can drop things into it
like cats and dogs
rats and snakes; children
make interesting sounds as well
when the lid is closed

When you drop a piano
it makes a sound -
the last chord in the day in a life
perhaps
When they are dropped from
a few stories
amid the splintering noise -
a dissonant chord sputters
up to the ears
like a dying campfire
suddenly extinguished
with yesterday's coffee
The REAL magic comes when
you drop a piano from
a great height
or hurl it into the side of a
granite cliff
Then the sounds of Armageddon
mingle with notes being released
from the captivity of strings
held at bay for so many years
The tinkling avalanche as keys
unlock eternity's mad mystery
cascading into the valley below
One long
            cacophonous
                        de-crescendo
collapsing
from chaos into accord

Paper Heart

I.
Walking the brick path
at midnight
after the rain
I stop and stare
at poppies
their orange petals
wrapped tightly
against this cold night

You have pulled away from me
wrapping yourself in
orange petals
against the chill
that I have come
to represent

II.
The room seems foreign now
the bed where we made so many promises
so many declarations
so many plans
the bed where the sacrament
of my love was delivered
to your temple
was laid at the foot of your alter
the bed seems an unmarked grave
where the ghosts and I
cannot find rest

The air is pungent with sage
purifying the hollow
left behind by your body
your promises of love
hanging in the air like smoke
lingering still
even after the fires of passion
has been extinguished
stubbed out like an
angry cigarette.

III.
I cup my wounded heart
which I wear on my sleeve
protecting it from the elements
it is a paper heart
made of old, dry parchment
when I uncover it
the sun will turn it to dust
and the wind will scatter it
to the four directions

I will let it go when I am done with you
not before

PANHANDLER

He looked up at me
with the saddest eyes
that I had seen in years.
Above the din of the traffic
I swear I could hear
Lady Day's "Strange Fruit"
or was it
"God Bless the Child"?
These were the eyes
of ancient sorrows
borne on the backs
and in the hearts
of a thousand years of
depravation and
slavery.

These were the eyes
that had seen
one hundred years of
choking poverty
generations of lives spent
in some shack
far from the big deal-
twentieth century.

Yet his face was not angry
or brutal or vengeful
rather it was tender and angelic
and he beamed with
obvious joy when the guy
ahead of me
flipped him a quarter
as we exited the "Box".

I avoided his look as I unlocked
the car door
He paused, disappointed
then moved on
to melt the next heart.
Maybe I'm getting hard-hearted
scraping by in this city of heat-waves
and hot lead.
Or maybe I'm getting more choosey
about who I invest in
I figure a guy
with his pants on backwards
has passed beyond redemption
no matter how angelic his eyes are.

Oven

The moon
a twisted smile
hovers over
the harbor
there is no
breath
only heat
a terrible searing
heat
even at dusk
even as yellow
and burnt sienna
and red clay
turn to cool
shades of blue
even as lights
twinkle on
as lights dance
on the harbor
like so many
paper lanterns

The peace of this
moment is broken by
this insufferable heat
like a death-rattle cough
heard through
paper-thin walls
as you try to tenderly
slip it in

This is the heat
that robs desire
that incinerates creativity:
The improbability of
Ice sculptures
attempted near
the mouth of the
blast furnace.

THE PRETTY WHITE TEETH DRIP DEATH

One oh one A.M.
Pulling in from a long shift
The winding down process
Will I sleep tonight?
Or will I spend yet another night
jumping into and falling out of the arms of Morpheus?
My job is taking big chunks of flesh
out of me
My job is a happy shark
ripping pound after pound
from my bones
Why doesn't the shark
just swallow me whole?
(a delicate snack?)
Instead the shark is inspired
to play an impromptu game of
water polo
with my bloodied-yet still
living-corpse
Why must the shark play with me?
What am I anyway
merely a toy?
I try to be strong
but right now I couldn't fend off a
mosquito attack.

I am weary of this shark
who playfully harasses me
taking little "love bites"
out of the fleshier parts

When I am done with this job
and Doctor time has healed my wounds
I'm gonna look like a patchwork
quilt
or a map of all the railroads in
America

Gainful employment
it sounds good when you are
young and ignorant
but watching the shark swimming away
with a pound of your flesh
in its big mouth
grinning like Hitler riding through
the Arc de Triumph
grinning from savage
beastly hunger
grinning at the joke
because it knows that it's gotten

more outta you than
the lousy eight bucks an hour
that it compensates you for
your lost time!
Watching the shark swim away
with your pound in its mouth
with your blood drooling out
little red ribbons trailing along
behind
like some pink Easter bonnet
gone dangerously wrong
you know that slavery has been renamed
you know that you can do nothing
about the shark-
it's gone-
You've already been tricked
you've already been had
there is nothing for you to do
but go home and beat something
the dog
the kids
the spouse
your meat-
what's left of it-

So go home and crack something open
maybe a six-pack
and flip on the tube
and watch the flesh-fest
watch the other dumb S.O.B.'s
trying to fend off the sharks
and laugh at yourself
laugh idiotically at this moronic
nightmare of a bed we've made
Kneel down and pray to
Al Bundy and Homer Simpson and
laugh yourself to sleep.

One for the Old Man

I sit here in the dark
remembering
the years before
and the years after
but stopping just short
of the years during

I sit here in the dark
alone
stupefied by the memories
that rise like
smoke
from the ashes of the past

I think of you
embraced by the cold
arms of the earth
quiet now
so far beyond us all

You lived like you drank
bottom's up
drain it
"More!"
and let the chips fall
where they may.

Trained Monkey

He did the poetry dance
three times a month, regularly
and whenever he could get a gig of his own
With a cute little tin cup
and Bell-Hop's uniform
he would show up at
readings all over town
and touch the hearts
of all those present

Or at least touch something
you know how monkeys are

Pinto

For two days
I have seen the same
miniature pony
tied to a pole
beside the highway
I keep looking for the midget
guitar-toting caballero
to come out of the Taco Bell
all smiles
to ride off into the happy ending.

There Are No
Ready Made Hells
For The Tormented

How is it possible
to ignore
the beauty
which frames our lives
like a pantheon
of lushness,
a blvd. of dreams,
a buffet of savory delights?

How is it possible
to stumble
through
the world
in dumb ignorance
oblivious
to the natural order
living only to suffer.

The appreciation of life
has nothing to do with
living it.

Just as a single flower
can captivate our attention
distracting us from this
drab, gray world
so to
in the midst of
the festival of life,
Carnival,
can we see only
the sad, lost child
or the broken dream.

Life is indifferent to our comings and goings
It's a blank wall on which we throw some colors
Heaven or Hell
this is the world
of our creation
because *we* decide
what color it will be
painted today.

So grab your brush
and let's paint the town red, baby!

SOMETIMES IT SEEMS MY CAREER AS A POET
IS DYING LIKE TIMOTHY LEARY

With something to say
and many ways to say it
and many voices to speak it
as many and diverse
as there are germs
on this planet
we approach yet another
poetry reading
we assemble our huddling masses
on the teeming shores
of this
the greatest
poetic landscape
west of the great river
Styx
we bring our tired
our poor
our hungry
yearning to read
freely
we wade into the water
waist high
black like ink
cold like revenge
swirling like the angst
that spills into this room
from the metaphor-filled
buckets that we carry
unable to be succinct
and to the point

After prostrating before the
divinitine
enough times
we have learned the drill
like a recidivist
who knows how to exit
a car
how to be arrested
without being beaten
too much
we know the ropes
sign in
coffee
say hi to friends
find seat
and
wait
and
listen to crowd
listen to poets

listen to your heart
"Get out now, get out before it's too late!"
listen to bored audience
listen to drone
listen to Cappuccino machine
as attendant tries to run it
quietly
and listen to polite applause
and wait for minute hand to
move another click closer
to the next hour
and wait for
the next standup poet
slash
actor
slash
singer
slash
comedian
to take to the podium
and prey that he
or she
doesn't plan to make this
a night to remember
with some truly
awful crap about
excreta
feminine hygiene
a disembodied cock
spurting blood
some weighty and deeply
profound insight
that sounds like a fortune cookie reject
or the death of art as a metaphor
for some damned thing!

And then there's Timothy Leary
adorned with his death mask
face
in a liquid
test-pattern jacket
and he's hung
with an entourage that
would put Johnny Wad
to shame
and they're filing down the aisle
making a minor grand entrance
as old Tim gives us all
his best geezer wave

Some poor bastard
having waited two hours
to share his burden
with us

must endure
the inevitable
departure of the geezer
and his crowd
plus half the audience
and the rest of the ass-licking
poetry toadies
yet he will persevere
and survive this night
as will we all
because we
are on a mission
we are the disseminators
of the word
we are the writers of wrong
the guardians
the keepers of the faith
wherever children cry out
we'll be there
(taking notes)
wherever there is famine
and pestilence
look around and we'll be there
writing truly moving verse
wherever hearts are being broken
we'll be there
(handing out Kleenex
and Prozac)
Wherever there is injustice
and rebellion
we will be there
with words of inspiration
we will help man the
barricades
we will crouch behind walls and
hand the loaded weapons
to the idealists and thugs

We are poets
the voice of conscience
baring silent witness
to life's cruelty
life's beauty
we document the nightmares
of the workplace
of the home
the street
the heart
the cell
psyche
ego
id

THE ROOM AT THE END OF THE HALL

In her mind's eye
she is still a lady
young
supple
Standing on the corner
of Pacific and Seventh streets
showing a band of soft
white skin
between the thigh high
black vinyl boots
and her shiny
red mini.

In her mind's eye
she still has firm
bountiful breasts
held in place by a
black silk halter
The rabbit fur collar
of her camel-hair coat
caressing her cheeks
like a reassuring mother's hand

She was young, once
an entrepreneur
respected for her ingenuity
her services in high demand
there was always a place at the table
Bartenders always had a kind word
she had no need for pimps
or perverts

Nowadays Poetry lies on an old mattress
stained with the excesses of artistic abuse
She's let herself go
and she has *gone*
saved only by the fact that her room
is dark
even at noon
as dark as the maze of rank hallways
that leads the sad clientele
with their stained and crumpled money
to her door,
where they are queried, not by the Minotaur,
but by her bodyguards: Greed & Ego.
Being perpetually hungry
Greed frisks the gullible citizen
while Ego engages them in some
topical repartee:
"Mr. Smith! You're looking very fit these days! How're the wife and kids?"

Nowadays she has an army of pimps

raggedy Ann's and Andy's
scouring the streets and boulevards
searching the cityscape for
a likely candidate
"Hey Mister, you want a date with my sister?"
"You look beat, Mister, my sister will make you feel like a man again!"
"Poetry is your best value, dollar for dollar!"

Between clients
she dreams of her youth
frolicking on the shores of the Mediterranean
in diaphanous togas
her lithe body
silhouetted
by the setting sun
falling, exhausted, into the waiting arms
of Morpheus
lovingly watched by Sapho
to dream of winged freedom
and labyrinths and riddles
thousands of years away from
the room at the end of the hall.

T. A. B.

She pressed up against me and
gave me a big hug
"Hi Dog!" She had purred.
She was all hair and
tight everything
tight ass
tight jeans
you could almost read the
label on her underwear
tight shirt
plaid
with tight cleavage
and I'll bet her
mind was tight
and so was her cunt
her legs around your waist
tight
she shut her eyes tight
as she gave me a peck
on the cheek
Even her lips were tight!
And as she pressed her breasts
into me
her tight little nipples
jabbed me like accusing fingers
and I swear it was all I could do
to restrain myself
if nothing else but out of respect
for her girlfriend.
She slipped out of my feeble grasp
and moved over to be with her lover
As she walked away
The sway of her tight ass
in those tight jeans
held me
spellbound.

THE QUEEN OF VENICE

It's been a long time
since
       we
            met
and
       I
            fell
so easily
       under your spell
You
       fed
            me
your
       fruit
it smelled of
            jasmine
but
       it
            was
bittersweet
And
       as I
            fell
into
       you
            I knew
that I
       would
            descend
still
       even
            after
you
       were
            long
gone.

THE OLD DOG

When the day comes
when the final bell ends his last
round
when the needle scratches
the last groove
and the last exacta is run
then they can have him.

When the last cunt-induced
sleepless night is over
when the last drop of wine is drained
when the last hangover fades
then it won't matter where he's gone.

But until that time
let him raise a palsied paw
to the sky
and howl at the moon for all he's worth.
So what if the swaggering blowhard
has been replaced by a staggering old pup.

Leave him alone and he'll still amaze
us
with that
one
last
perfect
gesture.

The Man Who Painted Birds

History's face
a simple canvas
muted with earthen tones
A sudden explosion
of feathers
shot through with color

The hand
a brush
The eye
a vision
Imagination
chronicler of beings: avian

A fist full of feathers
in the crotch of a tree
glued in place
by happen-stance
A sudden explosion of life
arresting the curious hard
The mad look of terror
and defiance

The flash point of a love
life-long and devoted
a moment of insight
congealing
becoming
passion
becoming the canvas
becoming the man.

in memory of Roger Tory Peterson, not just a painter of birds

La Puerta Del Diablo

Estoy triste hoy
La luna sonrie como un gato
Y me estoy ogando
Como si estuviera amarado con a stone
As if el Diablo
Abriera la puerta del infierno
Y me estuviera chupando
Dentro del vortex.

Que lastima!
Tengo un palo pero
No marshmallows!

Translation:

I am sad today
The moon is smiling like a cat
And I am sinking
As if I am tied to a stone
As if the Devil
Has opened the door to hell
And I am being sucked
Into the vortex.

Bummer!
I have a stick but
No marshmallows!

The Cheapness of Life

The young kids are turning-
like rats trapped in a maze-
on themselves
killing each other
for tricycles
and other accoutrements
of their young lives
Or killing themselves
because it is so easy
because life means nothing
because they can't cope
with this brave
new world. . .
They strut boldly across the stage
composed and cool
A picture of studied toughness
and disdain
hard and mean
like nails and broken glass
like black ice
invisible and dangerous
But the ice is thin
and cracks easily underfoot
sucking them under
into the dark lost gone world-
the REAL gone
you-never-come-back-from-world-
of-no-more-dreams. . .
Some would argue that
it's the triumph of Darwinian theory--
Natural Selection at work
Maybe so
but I find it disquieting
and sad.
It was bad enough when the damn
adults were so free when
it came to passing around
pain and suffering but now
everyone is
getting into the act.

Nothing is sacred
anymore

*For the two kids who jumped off the cliffs at Point Fermin, ages
14 & 15-- 5/22/96*

Sunday Night after the Christmas Parade

I sit at the end of the bar
at the other end
a happy drunk
falls off his stool.
"Oops!"
He grins sheepishly
as he replants his ass.
The bartender calls Davie's Cabs
and tells them to hurry.
Next to me
two "good, ole' boys" settle
themselves--
they've just come from
a rodeo in Lost Wages
and they want to get the grit
outta their teeth.
One of them
a short guy in a John Deere cap
is trying to pick a fight
with the other one.
His partner
complete with cowboy hat and boots
keeps admonishing
"Now quit?!"
I wonder how long before
the inevitable fight breaks out.
The waitress catches my eye
and tells she's not feelin' too good.
"I just puked in the can."
(thank you for sharing!)
I look down at my Chilli & Cheese Fries
"Does this look familiar?" I ask
holding up the basket
She goes green and makes
for the "powder" room.

Earlier in the day
I stood on the sidewalk
with the rest of my San Pedrons
watching an old fashioned
small town
parade
complete with marching bands
fire trucks
equestrian teams
even a Santa and reindeer team
pulled on a flatbed trailer
courtesy of the local B.P.O.E.

Unlike the previous year
where the "parade" lasted

about a minute and a half
and ended in that terrible
pileup at the bottom of
Sixth street--
the Pedro High marching band
sandwiched between the fire truck
and the electric trolley--
this year there was an air of actual
anticipation
as families crowded the parade route
and children swooped
and squealed along the curb
It was a real
"Norman Rockwell" event.
Even the Mayor of LA was seen
riding in a classic car at the start.

In the end
vendors pulling carts loaded
with "joy" followed
that same electric trolley
down the street.
A juggling clown
could be seen chasing
several teenaged pick-pockets
down the sidewalk
and bringing up the rear
a woman toting a battery-powered
guitar amplifier
while a cleancut guy with a
microphone preached fire
and brimstone
to the departing masses.

Later
two vagrants
with faces pressed flat
against the tavern glass
waited along with me
for a fight
to break up the monotony.

Thanks for the kiss.

It was like
slipping
into
    the
          pool the first time you go skinny dipping
all that warm yielding
that wave of wetness that cries out to you to
just keep sinking
until you disappear forever. and if not forever,
for a little while, then.

I'm sure that men
have done many stupid or
courageous things for the
likes of
    such a kiss.

wars and much drinking,
no doubt.
I wanted to stay there
longer, there
where our lips gently rocked
like seaweed doing the slow dance
with the tide, but the great desert of my loneliness
would swallow us up.

STREET OPERA

You see them everywhere
the flotsam spewed out of the
sewage vents of the great Technological Age
They go through the motions
trying to act like human beings
some making it
some failing but going about it with style
(playing a jaunty tune even as their ship goes down)
some failing miserably,
with no class at all
They wander the streets
like a troupe of psychotic Shakespeareans
acting out their particular brand of madness
Their performances start
anytime
anywhere
for any reason
They speak in tongues as knocked-out as
any Elizabethan dialect
Their costumery- bordering on tasteless -is something to behold:
a cornucopia of gypsy, vagabond, thrift-store-throwaway and
halfway-house-hand-me-down
The members of their troupe swelling and shrinking
in direct proportion to the political climate
A barometer of these halcyon days
Casualties of this rush towards
the Technological Godhead.

Stranger in the Bathroom

Once again
a stranger is in
the bathroom.

Bare feet moving
tentatively across the carpet
towards the bedroom.

Smiling widely
you accept the gift of my body
and I accept
the gift of yours.

Will you stay long enough
with me
to cease to be
a stranger
to my house,
my walls,
my heart?

SPEEDBALL

Where's the angle?
I can't find the angle
I'm starving
within this opulent facade
the glory shines
around me
through me
but I cannot taste
anything
I cannot read
what's not written
Cannot ride
on the wind
I'm no bird
Get me?
I want to see
beyond this grey sea
I want to sail away from here
Give me a torch
so I can see
more clearly
the land I dream of
Push me into the chamber
Cock the hammer
point me towards the horizon
and squeeze me into
oblivion.

A WINTER MEDITATION

Strategically located between Wilmas and Avalon
we huddle between the sheets against the impending
and unvarying weather/gloom
It permeates every angle, every corner
imposing its will, the bleak winter
pinning me to the ground, its boot on my neck
like a brown-shirted oblivion Ed McMahon
taunting me with promises of wealth and
early retirement....

At night the harbor is surreal with cotton-candy fog
swirling above mastheads as red, blue and green
lights blink like innocent bystanders
caught in a hail of gunfire, like open-mouthed
guppies paying homage to the face of God
weirdly magnified and contorted
at the edge of their known universe
Or the lights dancing on the rippling black mirror
pulsing to the tidal ebb and flow
like so many paper lanterns floating out to sea...

Nighttime points of light scattered across the sky
like embers from an overturned bar-b-que
Lights that sparkle as if all buildings are encrusted with
diamonds, as if skyline was painted with neon
on black velvet, as cold night blue/black plays
counterpoint to gold outline of high-rise towers

Back at Land's End
thick, wet fog is enveloping stick and stone
like a thick, cozy, wool sock, being pulled over heel
of San Pedro, as sea gulls cruise above
scanning always for edible salvage amid the debris
of civilization...

Man stares at reflection/shadow self
rippling in pool, moon could look better, but
it is cool cruel daytime and moonface has hair
and teeth and crooked smile
Moonfingers tip bottle into mouth and black worms
tiny like arcing backbones, squirm and seethe
violently convulsing in murkiness, rising, falling
balling-up
and then, silence...

But the canvas remains the same: gray
it seeps into every waking thought, every mood
every gradual hope or dream
even the final curtain must fade through gray
to reach black, the long, cool slab of solitude
the gray-t beyond...

Red blossoms litter the bricks
leaves once green and vibrant with life
lay in brown, wet clumps soon to be brown dust
future nutrients for red flowers, as yet unborn
ashes -gray- to ashes
dust to dust
the cycle begins anew
rising from the grayness of each winter
each year a Phoenix, fresh and alive
flicks its wings and vaults upwards...

The inevitability of this annual resurrection
is denied in the stillness that lurks in the shadows
there is a "no vacancy" sign at the inn
and no good news will pass over my threshold
without a fight, without some form of arbitration
There will be no peace in the valley
no laughter in the banquet hall
no fire in the hearth
no love until
the wounded heart recovers and forgives
until the first tender shoot of trust
breaks ground...

Until then, blue sky and brown clay swathed
in muted tones, blanketed and wrapped in a shroud of
fog creeping stealthily amid the silence of expectation,
my companions and I, scarcely breathing,
awash in amazing grays.

Yellow Man Sleeps

A few days into a month
of rainy Sundays
I'm thinkin' of changin' my name to Sunny
So's ta get everyone off my back
for all the bad weather
that the little boy
has brought to the
southland

At night
the streets look as though
a fresh coat of varnish
has been poured on 'em
The streets are dark
due, I guess, to cutbacks
in the city budget
The man-made potholes
growing proportionately deeper
with each inch of rain

It's been so wet that even the hookers
are off the streets
leaving behind the truly
destitute
and demented
all of whom look like drowned rats
save one
Sleeping alone on a bus bench
his kit
a plastic covered pillow
a man in foul-weather gear
shiny yellow jacket
the hood cinched down tight around his
almost featureless black face
shiny yellow pants
black boots
While San Pedro nestles in warm
cozy beds
a crazy yellow banana dozes
on the corner of Seventh and Pacific
Hopper-esque under blackened skies.

While You Were Out
for those who made it back, from one who never left

In dreams
I suffered with Caesar
clenching my fists
and forsaking the sweet nectar
of Fante's Wine of Youth
La Raza!
and Huelga!
Joan Baez
and the UFW
persecuted by angry Safeway managers
for upsetting shoppers, while
fighting the 'good' fight
WRL
SDS
CO and a lottery number of three hundred-something
no bed pans for me
marching still against jungle madness
against military-industrial-complex
SanFran
LA
Oceanside
being spat upon by self-righteous jar heads
debating the war at Loyola University with
my right-winged, hawkish history teacher
who went up the hill with TR
and packed a gun during the Watts Riots
(now sanitized into political correctness as the
First LA Insurrection- - uncivil disobedience?)
Taking a stand in '68
against the black and white horror
and still watching the TV show "Combat" religiously
the images of one war blending with the images of another
Taking a stand in '68
that still dictates my actions today
Choosing to fight with Caesar and MLK
anonymously
no recognition
no acknowledgement
shamed by the idealists who became idiotic consumers
as soon as the last helicopter cleared the roof
a generation of protesters
who flooded the free market with
their dreams of "thing-ism"
Taking a stand in '68
like Superman:
to fight truth, justice and the American way

We Are the Whirled

The next millennium
is sweating nervously
at the front door
like a over-anxious
first date suitor.

The next millennium
straightens its tie
and wipes the beads of sweat
off its forehead
with the sleeve of its coat
(a coat it borrowed from father time).
It checks its watch
and realizes that it's early
It's four minutes to the year 2000.

While the next millennium
nervously waits to knock on our
collective time door
(it doesn't wish to appear to be too eager)
we are systematically
whirling through the house like
the 'white tornado'
cleaning everything in sight
and making sure that all traces
of the last millennium
(who is just trying to get out through the
bathroom window-
but has gotten stuck!)
are gone.

The Millennium knocks
once.
OH GOD!
We're just not ready yet
so we rush even faster
even though we've still got
over 1300 days to go
Though I suppose a day is nothing
to a millennium…
nothing at all.
We know the measure of a day
even as that measure slips away
and there's never enough time
to get everything done!

And to my dismay I realize
that our little whirling dervish of a lifestyle
threatens to catch us all
up in its hands and push us

half-undressed to the front door
for our rendezvous with destiny
but there's no time for that to happen
'cause we got to keep running and
whipping everything into ORDER
cause the NEW millennium is almost here
and there just isn't any time for screwing around anymore!

And time
like a four year old brother
is constantly underfoot
innocently throwing obstacles
into our path:
unpaid bills,
sick computer systems,
threats of a gasoline shortage.
No matter what we do
we can't seem to get up to speed--
there is never enough time to get *everything* done
The moron in the car in front of you
never seems to drive fast enough
yet is able to anticipate your next move
and the guy behind you
never understands why you can't get the guy
ahead of you to get out of the way.

ESTA VIDA LOCA

A man dressed
in a tattered
evening suit
seat shiny,
derby
solicits customers
in front of
the Velcro Lounge.
A piece of cardboard
strapped to his brim
says he's
"BOB THE BALLOON MAN"
beneath this
in smaller letters is the explanation
but I cannot make out
the words
He is turning his attention to the crowd
at the bus stop
as I pull away from the corner.

A featureless guy
on a motor-scooter goes by
two unicorn-like horns
twist out of his helmet
his goatee is parted
by the 20 MPH
wind.
Even the devil
wears a helmet
these days.

A group of young men
"hombres malos"
cross the street
walking the
"BAD"
walk
they look remarkably like
Penguins in baggy denim
They never smile.
I try not to
make eye contact.

A white woman
heavy
with a sad
melting face
and a mangled arm
struggles
with a lifelong demon

I've been told that she was
interned in a Japanese concentration camp
during WWII.
An Asian man
sits comforting her
his delicate hand
stroking hers
in a miracle of
redemption.

A young man in cut-offs
pushes a shopping cart
full of junk
along the street
His dog follows on a leash
made of rags
He has been
"on the streets"
for awhile
no one seems to notice
or care.

Why are we not disturbed
by these strange turns of fate
Hair "systems" for women with
"mystery" thinning
"Wound Centers"
for that problem wound
that refuses to heal
The S.S.I. financed
underground economy
of dumpster diving
recyclers
stumbling through the streets
more ragamuffins
than men and women.
The populace
looks but does not see
the zombies are
taking over.

Your senses slowly,
methodically dulled
while you sleep
as if some dark power
had invaded your soul
and accelerated
the decaying of your moral nature.

WHEN THE LAST TEAR FALLS

It was another sad victory
for angst and pathos
She swears through tears
that she loves him
but she doesn't understand
why he treats her like dirt.
Tears roll down her cheeks
from her blinded eyes
and we both know that
there are many more to come
before the blindness will
be washed away
before she will see
what she has become
what THEY have become.

In the silence of this August afternoon
As the heat oppresses us
and her weeping
coats everything in this room with
a thin layer of sadness
I wait with her
for the last tear to fall.

Wall to Wall Emptiness

So it ends
not with a whimper
                    or a BANG
it
  just
     fizzles
           out
              laying
                    down to die
like an
old
dog

My space is reclaimed
no more panties hanging
from the towel rack
drying
no more soft nakedness
wandering through my _fe
like a field of
mad
orange
poppies
exploding
no
I am back
to my comfortable
uncertainty
alone
in this cathedral of dreams
where the walls
           stand straight up
                    and stare blankly
                         back at me
                              like cows
                                   waiting on

                                        the man

I thought I was

in trouble when
I couldn't seem
to write a poem
But then one
morning I woke up
and realized that
I couldn't keep it
up any more
And *then* the
poetry came!

He needed an excuse

to move on and she walks
down the stairs through the
room and out the door
and he says to his wife there
goes the best years of my
life that never happened
she looks at him as
if he's crazy says go
ahead you old goat chase
that dream down until
you've ground it into bits
and you want to come back
here but there'll be nothing
left for you at this address.

Goodbye Margaret Mead

In a moment of desperation
I sold half of my library to the local used book store
It was a rash decision for which I will
feel guilty the rest of my days.
I felt as bad as if I had given my
children away
just to put a few morsels of food into my fat little mouth
A meal can sustain a hungry belly for a few days, at most
but a few well written ideas can sustain a hungry mind for years
(what exactly is the calorie to word ratio?)
Now when I go in there
and see copies of my old books
it's like visiting the orphanage where my
soon-to-be adopted children
now live.
Slowly
they are being purchased and
given new homes
where they will be honored
and cared for far better than I ever could.

In this life of "Cash & Carry"
selling books to buy food isn't much of a crime
but this is little consolation for me
as I wonder where all my children
have gone to.

Playing At The Edge Of The Grave

Jesus hangs around in the hallway
at the foot of the stairs
weeping, maybe, weeping, yes
for all the lambs,
the children,
who lost their innocence
on their way to the adult-hood.

Jesus
last seen
in the bedroom
where goodnight prayers
are nightly made before
the descent into
the cool night begins
before the call of
Third Street
drifts into windows
disguised as Buddha's breath
So sweet and innocently it calls:
"Come out and play
con mi hijo
Come out and join our
merry band of Angels
and *play*."

Jesus loves the children
in the Buddha-hood,
growing up on the edge
while their parents are distracted
by a thirst for possession
and the hunger for status
- always in the name of the children -
Jesus knows their sorrow
their longing for the love-actions
not just the love-words.

Jesus hears their tiny voices in the night
and wants to carry them away
to heaven's eternal safety
But Jesus must wait
patiently
for a mother's distraction to blind
protective eyes -
for a fraction of a second,
just a short breath -
the careless child will come
the careless child always
miss a step while playing
at the edge of the grave,

and Jesus will be there with
the hand of guidance and redemption
ready to catch them as they flutter
like fallen angels
like leaves dropping from the tree of life
dropping into his waiting arms
waiting to lead them to their new homies
"En la vida loca".

In the town where I live
like your town and towns everywhere
there are graves.
Not ordinary graves with little markers
and flowers and the other commemorations
that loving families place on them to mark
the passage of time, the memory of their lost one's going.
Lord there are plenty enough of those graves!
But these graves are empty!
They wait like pot-holes on the road of life
wait for someone to fall.
for someone to slip out of line --
they are little traps
for the innocent and the naive.
They are the neighborhoods that have been written off
whose inhabitants have been
pronounced dead, though they still walk
and talk
laugh and cry
The City Council does not care
The Police do not care
The Church does not care
No one cares
They serve no purpose except as justifications
& rationalizations for why nothing can be done
why there must be more money
more police
more laws
more excuses
more votes
more fear
more bullshit
more of everything for some
and more of nothing
for those on the edge
of the grave.

WORK GLOVES & THREE-PRONGED ADAPTORS

A single work glove
lays abandoned
in the roadway

Its thumb pointing skyward
as if to say, "All right,
job done!"

Somewhere its mate waits
forlornly, perhaps in a tool bucket
or tucked into a work pouch
or carpenter's belt

Somewhere
some big lug with sweaty brow
and stained t-shirt
with dirty and calloused hands
searches vainly for a *pair* of gloves,
curses and heads for that pile
of splinter-infested lumber
unprotected
knowing full well that his number
is about to come up

Somewhere in space
there's a repository
for gloves and three-pronged adaptors

DISH WATER ANTHOLOGY

The morning coffee
is almost as black as the
dirt under my nails.

If Fruit flies could chuckle
then my kitchen would fill with
their joyous laughter.

This grim task set in
this dimly lit space, only
occurs now and then.

In hot water again
more an exercise, not a
moral dilemma.

Kitchen glows with a
dull warmth, nails clean but flies
now hungry and sad.

Suddenly This Becomes a Task

Just writing down the
anything
becomes an arduous job
Suddenly
without warning
the lights just wink out
and you wake up in a pool of sweat and shit
Suddenly
you feel your throat tighten
but you are alone at your desk
Suddenly
a cockroach's death
reminds you of your own mortality
Suddenly
life is no longer a sport and
you realize that it's a very dirty job.

Cry

Mercy
and
level
me
with
your
Dresden
eyes

Confirmation

"...it was the kind of
song where she'd
let everything go
& the dark places
in her voice let
her sing to the
heart of the river"
(Todd Moore - A Hotel Education)

Phrases plucked from the depths
of hearts unstrung
touching us
calmly
before doubt
turns
off the sound
and fear slams the
door again.

The Vengeance

Listen
You can almost hear them
Down on the flats
Tucked away
Inside the darkened doorways
Down the long halls
crouching in the corners
Planning the next move
The Avenging Angel of Death
With a rosary
And a shiny new gun.

BITTER PILL

In my new capacity as editor
and reviewer for the LUMMOX Journal
I now receive a growing number of poetry books,
chapbooks, sheets of loose poems, CDs and other
inanities related to the craft of poetry
and I don't always think about
or compare my own style to these
writings because I know that I'm a good writer, as well
and I'm secure in my place in the world...

But every now and then
I come across some other writer
in this case (writers)
who I feel akin to and I become
jealous of their success
and I wonder why I can't win a chapbook contest
or get a prize for my poetry or short stories
or why my asshole opinions aren't
lauded on high by the L.A. poetry community
or why I'm known for my rep but don't know what it is...

I'll be laying in bed reading, reviewing or editing
(much like Hugh Hefner, only I sleep with poetry and
he slept with pictures of women -- same theme, different jerk-off)
and I'll be thinking
Hey! I'm as good as this or that bozo! So how come I can't get a break?
And I read about apartments filled with furniture and love and light
and I look around me at my assembled trash/treasures
and I think that maybe I've miscalculated the formula for success
and maybe I'm lucky to still be able to tie my shoes
or hit the toilet without really aiming for it or having to concentrate
that hard on getting the food from the plate into my
black-hearted and jealous little orifice...

So, I brew the coffee the blackest and bitterest that I can stand
(or, at least that my colon can stand)
and bite the bullet
and forge ahead, with as much style as I can muster
It's another day on the line for some
another day in line for others
another day to be lined up and knocked down
Out there, somewhere more great poesy is being constructed
written without effort or reworked until it screams completion
Maybe I'll be writing it
(tho the odds are not in my favor)
But the chances are very good that I'll be able to read it
that it will arrive in my PO Box for my perusal
amid a stack of other lesser works
all wrapped in plain brown paper like
orchids among the onions...

BAD NEWS

I knew this woman
recently
a lovely creature, really.
I fell for her in a big way
got light headed whenever I
was in her neighborhood.
But there was one small problem
and she wore it on her
left hand
so I had to stay away;
on account of my
being bad news.

I've always been bad
news and have
been told to stay away
by many fathers
and even a few mothers
but mostly it's
the women who say
"leave me the hell alone!"

- Go away
crawl back into the
swamp you slithered
out of
there's a rock with your
name under it
yer ugly
yer stupid
yer bad news
do us a favor:
die now
avoid the rush...

This is what I think
about, sometimes
when it's late
like now,
I think about
a beautiful, young woman
swallowing razor blades
one, two, three
because she knows
about being bad news

Her memory is my razor blade.

6th & Mesa, Halloween

White gulls like bits of confetti
scatter overhead
seemingly startled by
blue sky and jet's traversing
path.

The postal mouth accepts my offering.

Travelin' Man

He brought into focus
the road
those byways and highways
that link us together.
He traversed the
north
American
continent
so often
that he knew the best places
to be in just the right
season
at just the right moment
to see the best
sunset
or catch the first
bird in flight
or celebrate the
wildflowers blooming

for the first time ever.
In chapter and verse
he brought the land
and the people alive
and each Sunday, he
brought the world
to us
the world and *his*
America of roads
and people with good hearts
and good dreams for the future.
He brought us tales of
hardship and hard work
of the rewards of perseverance
and of that damnable Yankee
ingenuity.
He brought to our attention
the nobility of the American Ideal
of freedom and truth
through the eyes and words of
American artists and writers,
of factory workers and civil servants,
of farmers and jazz pianists,
of musicians and dancers
and most importantly
he reminded us of the glory of
our oft-forgotten gift of life
by bringing the land to us
in all its stark, unadorned, and
un-enhanced beauty.

Willie n' Jack may have written
about it, but he

lived it
on the road.

Charles Kuralt (1934 - 1997)
(I cannot speak for anyone else, but I doubt that I am alone in this thought: his
constant presence served as a beacon, or a signpost, as it were, for a people who
have become increasingly lost in the latter half of this century. Charles Kuralt
continually reminded us of our humanity and of our potential as caretakers
of this place we call home. I have missed him since he retired from his post as
anchor on the Sunday Morning News on CBS, and now that he has retired
from this place we call home, I know that I will miss him even more terribly
than before. "Country road take me home..." adios, amigo.)

Crooked smile

over Lancaster
creases boiling
pink shrouded
thunderhead in
the northern desert.

One hundred miles
away, I watch from
the Gaffey turnout
and wonder how
I'll make the rent.

AUNT RHODA'S LAST REQUEST

My dad's brother
my uncle John
is going to drive from Arizona
to the Grand Tetons in Wyoming
(near Jackson Hole)
to scatter his wife's ashes to
the winds.

It was her last request.

After years of following him from one
"hole-in-the-wall" to the next
(all over the western states)
she's finally going to get him to do
something for her
(Besides take out the trash).
It's so romantic and
so much a part of the western tradition
like the last scene in the movie
"The Searchers" starring the Duke

I get a lump in my throat every time I think about it.

ROLLER

The fluorescent light buzzes
overhead with the certainty
of molecular physics.
As each day bleeds across
this calendar of dreams.
Clouds lurch across the
horizon like bumper cars
in heat.
Ten square miles of parking
spaces wait indolently
to be repainted.

The beautiful people risk
skin cancer and
the lunch truck is late.

Recipe For An Agonized Death

Take a bullet
The bigger the caliber the better
And glue a BB to the center of the casing
Then place the bullet between your teeth
with the business end pointing into your mouth.
Now bite down as hard as you can
Find a spot that looks very solid
And fall on your face.
Do this until the job gets done
or until you drop the bullet
(or swallow it)
or black out.
You may also try running headlong into
brick walls, or other hard surfaces
until you succeed.
Good luck.

Raft of Morphine

Photographic images mix
with memories and recent occurrences
forming a scrapbook montage
in my mind's eye, a constant
source of distraction
everyday, but even more
appreciated on this day,
day of waiting,
day of passage, perhaps, or
merely day of floating closer to the edge.

You lay sleeping on your raft of morphine
drifting in a cool white fog
towards the end of the world
towards the rim where the waters of sleep
spill over into oblivion.

I cannot be with you
dare not swim in those waters
out to your raft.
but I am with you in spirit
floating with you
my hands resting on your
sleeping form, as if touching
would make such a difference,
as if being there would matter.

It cannot matter that
there is a hard spot in my chest
or that I am so sad or
that I would choke on my tears
if I could see you now.

Only this fact that I honor
my memories of you
that I will always see you
as I saw you ten years ago:
my father's older brother
and my uncle Jim, a man
I respect
only this will matter
and only to me.

But I must let you go now
I can hear the roar of the water
it's deafening and yet, it comforts.

You drift on, then, and
good-bye

YO QUIERO

To live in a city
free of monsters

To escape the wonders
of man-made artifacts:
diamonds made from shattered windshields
armor piercing arrowheads
spent bullet casings
the ceremonial Styrofoam cup
the sacred cigarette butt
the droppings of bipeds
and pools
and pools
of gooey, black oil

To see the mountains,
standing proudly around us
no longer hiding in shame
behind a curtain of smoke

In short-
I want
To release
our city
(and our people)
from the captivity of fear
To feel, again, the pride
of being an Angelino
and a human being
creative and alive.

A Place In The World

A sweet sounding idea:
someplace that
can't be taken away
a room, a chair, a window
a tree, a hill, a patch of sandy beach,
a chunk of rock, a seat in the cab of a rusty truck,
the loving arms and lips of someone who cares
no matter what the crime,
eyes that light up whenever you visit,
a happy voice on the other end of the line,
a friend for life,
a vision of trees racing with clouds
over a stretch of dusky brown hills,
a knowing that you are
home, at last

a place in the world

a place
in the
world

THE PEACE OF BROKEN GLASS

The peace of a fluffy pink cloud
is really the peace of razor wire
I am hungering for some
tasty, warm little places
where the sun shines and
no one will ever bother me
'cause no one knows I'm
there.

When you look into my eyes
you cannot know how hard it is for me
not to run away from you.

You scare me.

But I must pretend that I'm here
even when I am not   Even when I am not here
I am.
I'm chasing my own tail
on purpose
It's all I know how to do
It's what I'm good at.
Don't bother me
I'm really busy
right now
I've almost got it.

Something Overheard in a Dream

You are your father's son
you can't expect much
so
don't
and you won't be disappointed

How can I argue
with such wisdom?

She wanted my happiness
and taught me how to
live on scraps
as if she had seen what the future
would bring
as if it had been revealed
in dream-time
foretold in prophecy:
Expect little
and you won't be disappointed.

And I wasn't

OTHER WOMEN

I have reached that age where the older women
whose company I once sought (because it made
me feel more mature) now all remind me of my
mother and the desire to go to bed in the grave
each night puts me off so badly that I can't stand
the sight of them the next morning.

Now I'm caught in a kind of no (wo)man's land
where women my own age aren't interested in
me because they recognize a true untamable
bachelor and they're too old to want to have to
break in another man; and the younger women
only want to be with me long enough to fuck
"daddy" out of their systems.

It's an interesting turn of events.

I wanted the thirty year contract complete with
kids, mortgage, etc. But what I got was twenty-
seven years of memories of other people's lives,
wives, and families.

One for the Poets

10 a.m.
and it's still so dark out that
the house cricket continues
its measured cadence of chirping.
I load a cup of day or two-old coffee
into the microwave and hit the buttons:
Beep, beep, beep, beep, beep
It whirrs gratefully.
Upstairs, I'm working my way through the last pages
of a book of poetry.
It's slow work
So many words
the messages are not always clear
The final days
the wife and the cats
sad faces at the track
famous names
The waiting.
I'll switch to another collection
written by a man and his wife
both admirers of the first writer
both stunned by his death
both good in their own right.
And I'll think about all the good writers that I know
all inspired by this first writer
all good in their own right
and wonder
about the point of this exercise,
this incessant tap tap tapping
that produces the words
that celebrate the ritual
of living
of dying
and all that lays in between.

ONE FINGER AT A TIME

Flipped off by a carload of
young anglo boys
while avoiding an unannounced
right hand turn
swerving into the left lane
coming down Gaffey hill at 22nd Street

Their anger
burning like dripping steel under
the welder's torch
lasted all the way
to 9th Street where they let up
and headed off towards L.A.
and some other brand of trouble.

I've been in this bind before
but learning my lesson then
did not push this one
farther than it needed
to go.

Driving has become as easy as
dancing in a minefield.

OASIS

With the strains of a Judy Collins song
rolling through my head
you know that one about
how her "father always
promised me that we would
live in France"
I lay in bed thinking about
my brief affair with Yvonne.
It's been close to ten years
since I saw her last,
a wistful memory
like that wistful song,
so I figure it's safe to
talk about her now
on account of how she's
left her husband and was
last heard from in Oakland, CA
where she was practicing the
Art of Gris Gris, making voodoo.
(Maybe it's not really safe
but I hope she'll understand)

I remember how she'd show up
at my mother's house and while
mom was away at work we'd
make love in the spare room
(what used to be my sister's room
before she converted it into a
dining salon, complete with chandelier
and a table big enough for ten)
and I'd watch as our bodies joined
together as I began to move inside
Yvonne and the afternoon sunlight
would spill through the window
across her upper torso, bathing
her breasts and neck and shoulders
in a swatch of bright yellow
and Yvonne would wrap her legs around
me and pull me deeper into her
as she began to come, her head
dangling over the edge of the
bed while I kept going, no need to rush,
rolling along like old man river
until I, too, would spend deep in
her valley.

And the last thing I would see
before closing my eyes would be
her smiling face, serene and care free
in that moment.

NORA PUSHES INTO AMERICA

With some uncertainty
I begin to write again
after a long absence
after contemplating
the desperation that Ernesto might have felt
I pull back from the edge
back from its seductive call
back from the sweet music
of destruction
"easy boy"
let go of the accelerator
let the speed fall away.

Nora pushes her way up the coast
knocking the shit out of tourists
& towns
like Jesus in the temple
uprooting commerce
No mercy this time

Nora swirls like a Dervish
and heads for Arizona
but she could change direction
and swerve into CA
just as easily
Nora is undecided
and we are nervous

We long for her promised
sweetness
long for her bounty of
moisture
can anything penetrate this angry
orange fist of ozone?

Can we get some relief
some respite from this angry fist
of heat?
Nora pushes towards us
redemption in her hip pocket,
her eye on el Norte.

MANGLE WINE

Orpheus descended into hell to save
the sweet Ophelia
who'd been invited
to disco
for all eternity with the devil until
Satan
got a glimpse of the
voodoo
under her toga
And started warming her up for
the horizontal tango.

Satan
plied her with compliments
about her ability
to accessorize
and made her head spin
with a suggestive
monologue about mangoes.

Ophelia
suddenly parched at one end
and moist at the other
requested
some refreshment
noting that Hell
was a truly hot and
happening room.

Satan
grinned a smile that made
nations weep
and swizzled a little
something
extra
into ol' Ophelia's glass
that made her want to
dance
like an angel

on the head
of his pin.

Satan
was only too happy to oblige.
By the time Orpheus arrived
Ophelia
was into the ninth chorus of
"Give me your swizzle stick,
Daddy!"

Orpheus descended into Hell
looking for his
sweet potato.
But man!
What he got back
was some spicy Cajun' fries.
Sho 'nuff.

Lost Highway

I can see it now
like a bent and crumbling
photograph
black / white tones
fading to sepia
"Ashes to ashes"
it always returns to the dust.

Brown like a field hand's back
soft like the dirt beneath
your toes, happy and wriggling like
tadpoles playing in a muddy riverbank.

Dirt roads suffering under
mid-August heat-waves
almost too hot for dust to rise
in salute to passing cars
or tractors or even the plop
plop, plop of a sway-backed horse
wearily returning its cargo
of two kids bursting with energy
- a summer paradox -
to cottonwood's shade
and swimmin' hole's cool allure.

Grouped around the sweating soda box
bottles of amber refreshment standing hip-deep
in cold well water, ready to be plucked
and guzzled, men lean into the shade of
the general / feed store, pressing into the
walls as if they could vanish if they tried
hard enough.

Men with faces harder than the walls that divide
the old South from the new, harder than thirty
days in the hole, harder than riversilt baked all
summer 'til it cracks like kiln-fired clay.

Men with lives as hard as any steel ever
to come south from Pittsburgh or Detroit;
Lives spent over a plow cursing a mule
working forty acres, a woman and a brood
of kids scrambling to raise a life up outta
the unforgiving dust of west Mississippi.

Men weaned on sweat and the sting
of the lash and the kiss of Jesus, slapped up
side the head by hunger, tornado, misfortune, desperation and still...

There is the easy laugh, the twinkling eye
a grin like the grillwork on a '49 Buick Roadmaster;
maybe just a touch of something sparkling
down in the ebony recesses like some

shiny bauble hidden away in a black bird's nest.

Through a patina of sorrow
resting uneasily over
these fields, this town , these people
the good-nature will not be suppressed;
It waits to smile sweetly at you from behind
Momma's protective skirt, wary yet curious;
It drifts seductively past your nostrils like
freshly baked sweet potato pie or corn bread
set out to cool on the window sill of your soul.

It's in the laughter of women
indistinct and joyous like a spring-fed brook rolling and tumbling with life;
in the twang of a guitar suddenly breaking the surface of a placid dance floor
like a catfish snatching a careless dragon fly;
it's in the rich, dark voice of hoodoo, Santa Ria,
the tail dragger, Chester Burnett, Muddy Waters, Fred McDowell, Sippie Wal-
lace, Ruth brown, Son House, Charlie Patton and Lightnn' Hopkins.

Across wooden floors
polished with age
with the naked imprints
of generations
across these cool boards
she moves
barefoot
the hem of her dress
dancing at her ankles
like a thousand birds rising to flight
reeling to and fro
flashing from light to dark
to light again
and still she comes
on feet as strong as
the desire to work this land
feet as brown as the soil
fecund and moist with life's
sweet potential
and still she comes
as if coming in from the fields
as if rising like spring floodwaters
seeking the crest
reclaiming what was once hers
and still she comes
proud and graceful
stately like a grand and noble cause
like an idea who's time has come
she has arrived
stand back and give her room

Now she calls the tune
she has come to *dance.*

Maturity

"Have you seen him lately!?"
She queries
Yeah, I say,
with his dye job tied in back
like an art fag ponytail;
his tight jeans and leather jacket
the zippers all magnificently chromed
as if the whole thing is preserved in a sealed vault
after each outing,
like Michael Jackson,
a sleeping beauty in a cryogenic chamber.
I'd fuck him myself if it weren't
for the repercussions,
I say
"You're sick" she chortles
As I recall it,
you did, on a regular basis
so, who's the sicker?
"Yeah. I don't know what I ever saw in that guy
I musta been lonely and desperate
Thank God I've moved on"
Yes, thank God
by the way, when's your boyfriend due for release?
"Next May"
she replies.

Yvonne's Blue Shirt

Yvonne wants to go to India
where the skies will come close
but never be her blue shirt.
Her blue shirt floating upwards
becoming for just one moment
a teal stripe on a flock
of ducks resting calmly
on the lake.
Her blue shirt obscuring
skin the color of the Ganges
after spring floods.
Her blue shirt at rest
calmer than a Calcutta sunrise.
Her blue shirt
a crumpled rag at the foot of the bed
without form or substance
just 100% cotton and dye.
Her blue shirt like
waves rolling in from el Pacifico
massaging her neck
encouraging a gentle smile.

India never had it so good.

VACATION

I'm trying to sleep in someone else's bed
It's not as easy as they thought it would be
Where I sleep, what I'm used to
it's more like a crypt that I crawl into
dark and cold with pillows like stones
my mattress is hard and flat, like a pallet
My windowless cell, with it's barred skylight
my dank prison calls to me to turn away
from the comforts of white walls, early morning light,
pale curtains and a wall furnace that happily
churns out heat as I stand naked in pre-dawn chill
marveling at the thin red line panorama:
Eastern mountains cloaked in blue,
a silver sliver of moon hung in pale blue-gray sky
the sea, an oily gun-metal blue.

It's hard to believe that I'm still in the same town.

First Feelings Upon Reading a New Book of Poetry

If it's good
there is a tightening in the chest
followed by a thickening of the air
as if one is awakening in
the moist, cool grip of
a hollow grave
as the last shovel of dirt is being tamped down.

If it is bad
there is a tightening in the chest
followed by a thickening of the air
as if one is awakening in
a Sunday morning drunk tank
with no bail
and one hardassed hungover Samoan
eyein' your ass.

If it's good
you resolve to hang it up
and never darken the door of your
writing room again

If it's bad
you resolve to hang it up
and never darken the door of your
writing room again.

If it's good
You realize that you must
keep going on
to fight the good fight
and defend the honor of the Muse
against all comers

If it's bad
You realize that you must
keep going on
to fight the good fight
and defend the honor of the Muse
against all comers

If it's good
you will be depressed for a while
a week at the most

but if it's bad
you will burn with an anger that will
stay with you for weeks
maybe even years.
It will burn in you like an atomic cinder.

I don't know which is worse.

TOO SOON

So much depends on
the grinning of a lone
child
laughing,
on the run
like Neruda's:
brown & agile,
at loose ends
with seaweed hair,
floating free,
unadorned.

A simple grace

Too soon
Too soon
the weight of anguish,
a carpet of lilies
on fields of Flanders,
Belfast, Soweto, Compton,
Sarajevo, Beirut.

Too soon
the tolling of the bell
Too soon
the world is
at once,
bigger
and yet (somehow)
smaller.

Too soon
the long night,
like a blanket,
covers us all.

*Inspired by the recent deaths of two young men whom I had known for
over twenty years, since they were 8 & 10 years old, respectively. Bart
Albright - Melanoma, age 32; Chris Sauvé – Heroin O.D., age 29*

THE STOOL

It sits in the corner
the stool
with its wooden legs
painted white

It used to be taller
but necessity made it shorter

It has three boards nailed
to its seat
the boards are old
(they were old when I
found them in 1971)
Now the boards are older than
some of my friends
as old as my last girlfriend was

The stool looks solid
It is a metaphor for myself
It looks solid
but it is not
It is loose in all its joints
and keeps falling apart
even as I put it back together.

It is one of the constants
in my life and has traveled
with me faithfully through
thick and thin
feast and famine

Girlfriends have come and gone
their memories fading like old
photographs like receipts from
all-night drug stores
only the furniture
only this piece of furniture
remains

Hell
it's even older than
the guitar I used to
seduce you into bed
and more reliable
than my best pickup line

THE POEM WILL SAVE YOU

"even their nightmares are ringed with tinsel"   Charles Bukowski

It's the middle of May and a warm tropical rain is falling
turning dusty streets into greasy ones.
I'm reading the newest book of poesy
from my favorite, now dead, poet
and marveling at his clarity and the strength of his lines.
He said it
"The poem will save your ass from madness"
The poem will save you
while fat drops of acid rain descend
while the bills pile up
while the paint peels
while you wait and wait and wait
for something to change
it doesn't matter what it is
as long as it's *something*
The poem will save you
while your auto insurance climbs
while the phone screams your name
while the pipe calls to you
from the other room
while your heart considers the pros and cons of retirement
while the babies scream for attention
while your mind begins to go
while lovers dream of each other
while you dream of becoming someone else
while hookers hook
and junkies junk
and the stoner gets steadily dimmer
while the whole county flatlines
from a bad batch of crystal
while the beer goes flat
while the women come and go
while you jerk into the hollow memories of their
brief laughter
while someone lets the air out of your tires
and the wind out of your sails
and the joy out of your days
while the life seeps out of your windows
and each breath takes you farther away from
life and closer into death's final orbit
while the warranty on your vcr runs out
while the internet sucks you dry
while the open grave waits patiently
and the orange waits to be peeled
and the lights flicker
and the ground moves
and the really important stories wait to be sold
and the needle crawls across the floor

at 3 a.m. like an inch worm
while you wait for it's promise of happy stupidity
while you binge on lollypop dreams of power and glory
while they plot the next turn in your life
while the streets are overrun with anger
and revenge
while you grab as much of the pie as you can carry
while the 911 call goes unanswered
while the oven begins to look very inviting
while you place a razor blade on your tongue
and swallow
while you eat all the right food groups
and still get cancer
while you starve to death
on a diet of empty promises
still-born dreams and low-fat hopes

The poem will save you
The poem will save you.

Karen

I dreamt of you
Your head cocked towards me
as if gauging my every
weakness
analyzing my vulnerability
to your charming ways
like so many years ago
after you left the hospital
your time of sadness
behind you
and mine
just
beginning.

The Bastards Are Waiting

In shadows
Under bridges
Behind bolted doors
Around the next corner
In the stockroom
By the dumpster
Near the water cooler
At the exit
Of the office
Of the airport
Of the driveway
On the median strip
In the next row back
Inside the entrance
On the next stool over
At the next locker
In front of you at the checkout
Behind you at the car wash
Above you at corporate HQ
Below you in the underground

The bastards are waiting
Everywhere.

A Snapshot -1981 -
Boy on Wall with Cat and Ball

I watched him transform from
the cockiness of childhood
to the uncertainty of adolescence
to the quirkiness of adulthood.

My young friend
impulsive, yes
a boy balanced on a wall
holding a cat in one hand
and juggling a ball with the other
ready to rip it up
at a moments notice

My young friend
goofy at times
silly at others
always with the answers
to hell with questions
no doubts
always the forward rush
straight to the top
all things possible

with age came transformation
and growth, altitude
the "Whatever!"
changing to
"Don't fuck with me!"
Consequences became reality
cause and effect no longer
an exercise in speculation
the boy on the wall
juggled life for real
playtime ending soon
a reluctant transition to manhood

Lonesome calls at midnight
planned visits that never
seemed to happen
too busy, too busy
to stop
and smell the coffee burnin'
The innocence of that time:
the boy on the wall

the cat, the ball
all gone
all gone

My young friend
gone now
sailing away
going down, down, down
the devil chewing on his leg
A final kiss from sister Morphine
Nothing left to do
nothing left
just a phone call
and a photograph
loves is real
and not fade away.

In memory of Chris Sauvé   1968 - 1997
"Gone but not forgotten"

SOS

I ran into one of my old girlfriends
at the corner table
where the whole mess began
She looked fine!
As usual
So of course I got ideas
Not because I still carry a torch
or anything like that for her
I just missed her lips
and her warm youth
spreading around me
like the laughing sun
on a warm, summer's day
But the present is never like the past
and what I got was sarcasm
and accusations
an unrelenting litany of "I know's"
and "You did's"
No kiss or gentle loving
is worth that
abuse.

Turning in the Silence

I am a reluctant gypsy

the lure of the road has little meaning for me
except that it defines the connection from
point A, my birth, to point Z, my death
and serves to mark the unraveling of my time
on this earth.

This one thing is true
I shall not care
who weeps for me
when I am gone
I shall not turn to see what is behind me
nor will I search the horizon
for my future

Like the passing of a season
on the tree of life
I shall wither and fall

Already I am turning
in the silence of Fall's
long, cool evenings

Saturday Morning Driveby

An old latino
at least
a white haired man
sits on the steps
of an empty lot
a nice house probably stood
atop these steps, once
but no more.
The man looks grimly
out at the street
as I drive past
He does not follow
my passing
with much interest
His face is as cracked and weathered
as the concrete steps
on which he sits
There is an easy sadness
about this moment:
The Man
The Steps
The Driver
The Street.
Nothing is required of
any of the players
only the simple movement of the day.

The Moth

against the window
the moth
intent on escape
wings beating
a blur of brown dust
at full power
eyes focused
on the prize
not comprehending

the moth
its mantra:
Try!
Try!
Try!

The moth
against the window
impulsive
alive
intent
pushing
beating
without a moment's pause
not grasping the obvious
wings a blur
nose flattened
against the odds

I think:
"the only difference between
this moth and me, the
only true separation is
that the moth still believes
it can escape
and I no
longer
do."

The moth
against the window.

McCoy Tyner at the Jazz Bakery (10/02/98)

The master of WOW
attacks the piano
with powerful hands
pounding out the melodies
like an artillery barrage
or the storm surge
advancing in front of
any "one hundred year"
in recent memory.

The master of WOW
taps a steady beat
while fingers hurtle
down keyboard
like a sprinter in the
one hundred yard dash.
Stabbing the ivories
like a shower of arrows
landing with the power of
lightning bolts
scattering notes like
startled birds.

"Bud" does not merely
walk in -- he kicks in
the door, pins you against
the wall and demands to
see some ID.

I'M FALLING

it feels so easy
effortless like
breathing or
the pumping heart
a "no-brainer".
I'm falling
like a feather
from God's wing
it is so easy
I don't have to do anything
I don't even have
to let go
"It's all been taken care of."

I'm falling
through space
not knowing
where from or
where to.
It doesn't matter
I'm at ease with this
(which is odd).
Acceptance was
never this easy.
.

I Look at Her

at the miracle that is her
I cannot look away
at least, not until the miracle moves on.
I notice a tear forming
in the corner of my left eye
I will not try to stop it
as it rolls southward, down my cheek.
"Why are you sad?" She asks.
I'm not sad.
It's one lousy tear that I shed
for this miracle that is this day:
for her silhouette against the window
for the birds I hear outside
and the rustling wind in the trees.
For the outside sounds as they
blend with the inside sounds:
the humming refrigerator,
Van Morrison crooning like an Irish Tom Waits
(in the Small Change years),
the click, click, clicking of the blinds
brushed by a slight breeze
that plays with her hair.
The peace born on that wind
smoothes out the wrinkles of my
troubled soul, whispers into my ear,
as this new day begins,
"This day might be different..."
Perhaps there is the promise of a new vision
as if my solo tear could cleanse and purify
like a benign corrosive
clearing my bedraggled head
and sweeping away the fog that obscures
my comprehension.
It is in the light of this miracle
that I see her
in this symphony of the senses
that I grasp who she is.

Horizon's Edge

Alone and half-naked in the early light
wrapping covers around me in the cold
morning, unseasonable in early April,
I'm struck with contrasts:

how your apartment hums with machinery
(the elevator at 2:39 a.m.
the whirring pipes next to the toilet
and that soft, disembodied clicking, as if
there are whales hiding deep in the basement)

how mine echoes with footfalls,
(as if the storm troopers are on the march again)
and the screams of children and their dogs

how your apartment smells of coffee
and citrus soap, of lentil soup and baked bread

how mine smells of stale cigarettes
(from the last tenant), incense and socks

how your windows open out onto a quad
of grass tufted with little white flowers,
cement walkways, and trees

how mine open to roof-tops and stucco
beneath line of sky, framed into thin vertical
lines by iron bars.

II. "Come to me"

Within the limited context of my life
I am unable to move in half measures
You murmur my nickname
as I descend into your domain
as I pluck, cautiously, at your heart-strings:
a piano tuner, caressing your ribcage
coaxing sounds from your depths:
giddy little arpeggios of laughter,
delicate, upper-register fingerings,
and crashing chords: left-handed waves
that churn your bed from safe-harbor
to open-sea, that push you to the horizon's edge

Where I, like a hungry sea-monster, wait to devour you.

His Brief Parade

We talk of dying.
He is creeping across that threshold
like a long shadow.
He has come to this portal
sooner than expected, my senior
by only a few years
cut down by a degenerative disease
called ALS.
"None of my male friends call
or visit me anymore, only the women," he says.
Mortality is a tough issue.
Men would prefer to go out
heroically or suddenly,
in a blinding flash
not slowly fading away
like an old piece of newspaper.
Women can stand the pain,
the protraction of it,
this is their territory.
They know suffering and its weight.
They bare it better than we do.

Of course, there is the possibility that,
as the millstones of death slowly crush
his bones into a fine powder, these angels
of mercy are gaining some small satisfaction,
some exactitude of revenge,
for all the years of suffering that he
has brought to their doorsteps
during his brief parade upon
this planet.

Still, one
hopes for some
forgiveness
and compassion
and a last angelic smile
before the end.

HATE/ LOVE

it's been a bad month
I had a string of bad dates
and then I met you

I wanted it to be like water
but it was like mud
clumpy-lumpy-like your face, mud
your breath was like fried eggs
on Sunday afternoon,
late Sunday afternoon
you moved into my life like
the Exxon Valdes that night in Alaska
you moved into my Alaska and broke open,
spilled
like a hundred open wounds
like the pain of a hundred rusty nails
driven into the palms of my hands
and then you got out the pliers, the vicegrips
your perfect little instruments of torture
and you said;
"Yeah baby, now I'm really gonna send you to heaven!"
And then

        you ripped out my heart
and you dangled it in front of my face
like a pair of red panties that you'd just found
in the glovebox
as if to say, "What's this all about then?"

        you ripped out my heart
and you squeezed it until it popped
like a ripened tomato

        You ripped out my heart
and dropped it still beating into a shoe box
where it lay quivering with your other trophies
of loves lost

        You ripped out my heart
and grinned like some demented Aztec priestess
radiant in the spectacle of horror that you created
intoxicated by the power that only you possessed
indifferent to my pleas for mercy

        You ripped out my heart
and you laughed gaily
and walked away

Girl In A Red Dress

At the Los Angeles County Art Museum
with my friend to see the time capsule
show: Harlem Renaissance
I came across the painting by Charles Alston.
The Girl in the red dress seems
very prim and conservative
looking off to the left and slightly
downward her face is otherwise
expressionless, almost inscrutable.
The other portraits look right at you
or through you, but the girl in the red
dress cannot look you in the eye
for some reason only she and
the painter knows.
Somewhere I saw a painting once
of a parody of American Gothic
with a black man and woman
in the places of the older white farm couple.
Neither of the people had faces, just
black silhouettes where their faces would
be. This was symbolic of the fact that
white America sees the black race without
a face, according to the artist who painted
this portrait. This painting was not
included in this show.
The girl in the red dress, her features
highlighted by red on a brown-almost black
head and neck appears thin and young
unremarkable in every way, yet
there is something there, something
stately and elegant, something that
makes me think of that song by Nina
Simone, "Four Women".

Four Short Poems

I thought
of suicide
until I
remember
ed the taste
of fruit

The sound
of Buddha's
voice lingers
in the ring
ing of the bell

Death comes
when hope
has faded
beyond
memory

The
blanket
of dreams
wraps us up
and carries us
away

Eyes   Like Mingus   (For Steve Fowler)

Eyes   like flint
like flecks of coal
like shiny bits of starless sky
trapped in the ruins of a slag heap

Eyes   like molten steel
sullen and angry
piercing -- a bullet finding its mark
like a jaguar
passionate and alive
yet hating the trap
pacing behind the bars
bars like a skeleton
trapped inside the mind
behind

Eyes   like Mingus
like notes caught in the net
like the grid of notation
like Mingus
in shamanic Mexico
trapped in a chair   .
no strength to grip
no fingers to coax notes with
no feet to stand up and count with
no time -- no signature

Eyes   like concrete -- shattering
like glass -- splintering
like the wrecking ball's slap
like voltage -- unregulated
like a passion laid bare
to the gallery's scrutiny
like the madman's frothing nightmare
like the inexplicable accuracy of random fate
like a shot to the belly
like Coltrane's "Favorite Things"
like your fingers -- stilled

Eyes   like an empty glass
staring bug-eyed into space
upturned and dispassionate
like a dream -- lost in the stars

Eyes   like Mingus
silent but never
silenced.

I Must Be Getting Older

When did taking a good
shit become my most
treasured part of the day?

Another Day

Memorial day.
The sun obscured.
Cloudy haze stubbornly
clings to the sky.
Air as still as the street.
I can scarcely breath.
Heat rises from a sea of rooftops.
Monotony hangs limply
a forgotten banner.
The sameness of each moment
uncoils and drops.
Sun crawls along the horizon
a lizard steadily heading west.
No magnificent vistas here.
Platitudes lay in the ditch
discarded tires only.
There are no bodies.
My secret eyes know where to look.
Sun rolls over the next hill.
Eyes closing
till tomorrow.

A tough weekend

It was the celebration of Labor
more than that
It was the celebration of the benefits of Labor:
Wine
Women
Song
in that order.

Kirosawa, the great Japanese director
finally sheathed his sword;
the great poetry entrepreneur
was still giving me dirty looks
his filthy black heart
pumping blood, amazingly,
instead of crude oil;
the Woman raising doubts
about the sanity of our involvement
(what does she think adultery is);
my father, a well-meaning old guy,
sends me a list of "items" from his brother's
estate, saying that I should indicate which
mementos I would like to have --
the Waring Blender catches my attention
but I suddenly feel like I'm casting lots
for Christ's clothing;
I go to see a "romantic comedy" with the
Woman and I'm confronted by a ration
of emotions that rise like a blister on the
backside of my memory, reducing me
to an emotional vegetable, which only
the raw passion of sex can save me from
and I *am* saved.
Roger Maris's record of 61 home runs
still stands as of this writing
as do I, which is something
if you think about it.

11:22

The first murmuring
that I remember of
the death of innocence
was the time when Troy Thorn
set his sights on me
and made me 'enemy for life'
Grade school got harder and
Junior High seemed an oasis.

The second murmuring
came in a California fall
a cool and cloudless day
delivered by our ancient
English teacher
paler than usual
lips quivering
the unthinkable silence
the room so quiet
afterwards
Stunned and uncertain
why this could happen
here in Camelot.

Troy Thorn was a foot
shorter by this time and
had found the glories of
a sock full of glue by then.
Unlike Kennedy
Troy ended up like Elvis
OD'd on the bathroom floor.

But each man was
influential in his own way
each man an obstacle
to be dealt with
to be overcome
each man a milepost
marking this passage.

Troy was rotten from the start
it was widely known
But Camelot, like the Great
Wizard of Oz, remained
enshrined in my memory for decades
A state of perfect grace
blissfully ignorant of the man behind the curtain
who as it turns out was as rotten
as Troy Thorn and his brother, Brian
combined.

Growth Spurt

I don't know
if it's a sign of
maturity or not,
but lately, I'd
rather jerk-off
than read
Bukowski.

New Dawn

Sleeping in the shadow of a ghost
I find little rest;
but with you
wrapped in my arms,
breathing in cadence...
I am, oddly, at peace.
Though it is early in our time together,
we seem to be already
woven together,
like the strongest Irish linen,
as if a master weaver
used a thread
of divine strength
during the night to join us

you are my warp
and I, your
woof

Without

TV speaks to anyone but
I don't understand the message.
There is a reason for all this
but I don't want to remember.
I think instead of the desert.
Or a pile of rusting debris
or a bleached boney thing
with feathers torn
from an oblivious sky
or of riverbeds laid barren
robbed of life by merciless fate.
Change tugs at my sleeve
begging me for mercy
but mercy has run away
with the circus.
The desert returns to my thoughts
a bullet riddled shack
the light spilling through
a shower of meteorites.
The miracle of high noon.
I want to lay down and sleep
through summer.
Birds of prey circle overhead
waiting the foolish mistake.
Perhaps the circus will
come back to town
once more

Touch Me

Touch me
and let the masks fall
from my harlequin face
like leaves collecting
at winter's doorstep.

Touch me
and unleash reluctant tears
as an uneasy rain
to absolve my sins
and wash away my
memories
of this paradise lost.

Touch me
and make me whole
my darling.

Touch me

Like the Wings of the Butterfly

The miner, Wang Shu Bin,
tells the story of his last
hours with his wife:
trapped within the rubble
of his hospital ward
after a devastating earthquake
"My wife called to me
in the darkness, we were both pinned
under debris, "Wang Shu Bin! Are you
alive?' I said "yes, can you move?"
She said, "I am pinned from the waist
down." I began to claw away at the
cement blocks that buried me. It took
two days for me to reach her. She
was only three beds away
from me. I tried to get to her but a large
beam blocked her from me. I could only
touch her fingers. When she realized I was
beside her, she was so glad, her fingers
fluttered like the wings of a butterfly.
For two more days we talked of our past,
of our love for each other. Throughout
her fingers touched mine, speaking to my
heart, directly. Finally, she said one word to me.
'Wang,' and the butterfly ceased to flutter.

The Road (More or Less Traveled)

Day's end and I'm
picking up pieces
of past lives
scattered across this plane
of memory.
It is an incomplete geometry
with angles so obtuse
they will not intersect,
the whys outnumber the ex's
and yet, they still add up to zero.
Day's end and I'm
unsure what the product is.
These calculations
should add up to sum-thing
but I'm not sure what its value is.
The road winds on ahead
of me, and even though I left
the station at four thirty and
have been traveling at sixty
miles per hour, I still don't
know when I will arrive

or, worse yet, where.

The Rain
The Rain
    Falls
    And Falls
        For Days On End

The rain falls
the room is tragically dark
the streetlight on the corner
creates a waterfall on
your face, blending
with the tears that
I know *must* be there

The rain falls
for days on end
and I know you must be
crying like that train
that I hear in the
distance, I am
mesmerized by your
Matisse-like face

The rain falls
and I long for you
but only your memory
lingers in the room
like an odd perfume
as still as wood

your face:
as the curtain of rain closes
around me
a liquid shroud
that will shimmer in the
light of a new day

The Patient Bed

The patient bed
waits within the darkened
walls of your apartment
waits for the end
of summer, for the
return of laughter
and the aroma of
fresh brewed coffee
drifting in at seven a.m.

The patient bed
with sheets pulled snug
waits in silence to
carry your body to the
arms of Morpheus,
arms that will hold you
and support you
while sleep caresses your weary
temples.

The patient bed,
a boat for navigating
the sea of dreams
lays moored to the nightstand
ready to set sail
with the receding tide,
waits for the captain
to return

The patient bed waits
for your return
as do I.

The Light Obscured

Once I saw a raft
drifting into the gray
mists of this world's edge
and I wondered if you
would understand what I
meant about the heaviness
in my heart or the sorrow
that held my face like
his tired hands might have
had they had the strength.
Now I think of your hands:
how they must be tired
how fragile they must be
fragile and transparent
like layers of mica and
old parchment, the light
obscured like frosted glass.
My vision becomes worse
as the light fades, as
sorrow becomes a shadow,
a dark shape disappearing
into twilight's gray curtain,
as you turn as if to wave.
But you do not see me
standing on this distant shore
and turn away, a perfect deja-vu.

Tank Farm

Lou was welding
on top of the tank
when a spark ignited
a ghost vapor
and blew him
clean in half.
I couldn't stop
shakin' for a week
so the company sent
me to Port Angeles.
Beneath the Olympic
Glaciers I finally
slept easy and
the coffee began to
taste good again.

Swallow

In the end
it is not the fire
that one fears
but the silence that
will swallow
the sun and moon and stars
and all the
memories.
Everything
will grow fuzzy
and lose all meaning.
I hope your image will
be one of the last to go.

There are no guarantees.

Table Scraps

Was it a misunderstanding?
A light breeze moves the curtain
in an afternoon memory
a long forgotten dream that rises and falls
an image of breathing, spoken to a lover
as our own breaths,
in silent metaphor for our innocence,
were woven together, twining
like two vines in tandem,
growing into and around each other.
I pause and study my hand:
it's ruddy skin and shiny calluses,
dinged and dented by manual labor.
I trace the outline of the scar
on my thumb, a trophy of some adventure
forty years ago.
I return to my mother,
in her own gentle way,
telling me not to expect much out of life.
Did I misunderstand her?
Thinking she wanted me to learn to live on table scraps,
like some farm dog,
to grow up tough and proud
never needing to rely on anyone for anything.
I think of how much like a little boy I am now,
how much I need right now,
how much I need to be scooped up and held.
Hold me in your arms, momma.
Don't push me away.

A light breeze like a quiet breath
plays with the hem of the curtain.
My hands begin to look old.
I wonder what miracle I will pull
from this junkpile
next?

Soutine's Palette

Encased in a plexi-glass display
at the LA County Museum of Art
is the last palette of the painter
Chiam Soutine:
two boards held
together by hinges so
encrusted with paint
that no trace of rust
decays their purpose.
The palette is a deep green
as if by some foundation of color
the painter Soutine might
create his lively portraiture
and fluid landscapes.
The palette is bordered on
two sides with fat globs of
paint: little mountains of muted
browns, reds, blues and yellows
that rise above that flattened
plain of green, colors that appear
dulled by stillness, unused
for nearly fifty five years.
We see the palette as *artifact*
with its border of knobby
paint waiting patiently for
Soutine's returning hand and
stabbing brush to awaken
the life that lays dormant
within the skin of its
mummified pigment,
waiting for his next
inspiration to summon
forth the magic of color
and light.

Saudade (for Monica)

Many people will walk in and out of your life,
but only true friends will leave footprints in your heart.

This is what you feel
when you wake up alone,
as you shower and dress,
as you eat a meal.

It is in the air you breathe
it is in the food you eat
the bed on which you rest.

No amount of "medicine"
alters this reality
no thing can dilute the
power of its presence.

It is atom on which
your universe is framed
the essence
the all
and the
nothing.

San Pedro

Yes, it's true, I left San Pedro
though in truth
it must also be said
that you can *never*
leave this town
entirely.
It will follow you
like a bad rumor
like a stray dog
like a dream never realized
never captured.

Even though I only lived here for 6 years
it felt like home to me.

But "home" is an uneasy concept
something always sought after
rarely achieved
"A place in this world"
a distant vision
a life glimpsed in passing
something that I've seen
or thought I've seen
but never been able to find
when I retraced my steps.

San Pedro has come the closest
in many years of that dream:

HOME

But the reality of dreams
is not always as grand as the illusion.

San Pedro was this as well:
the site of many disappointments
where the triumphs were overwhelmed by
the failures, where I found myself
and was dismayed at what I had become.

San Pedro, it's not just for breakfast anymore.

It's a way of doing
a way of being done
with a style all its own
this is the San Pedro that I'll
always choose to remember

Not the San Pedro of pettiness
or of feuding or backstabbing.

These things are everywhere
in every city
in every heart
they are the potentials
the possibilities.
These acts of smallness are merely obstacles
thrown up by the ignorant
by the fearful.
A minor irritant
like the beggars outside the Post Office
They CAN be ignored
but you have to want it
you have to want to
believe
in the possibilities.

I stopped believing
and this is why I moved away
into the the God-forsaken
wastelands of
Long Beach.

But
there will always be
a piece of San Pedro
buried deep in my
heart.
Of this, I am certain.

Old Paint

Spanish Mike
sat on the tailgate
of his pickup and
waited for
the dustcloud to
reach him.

The pickup, an
ancient, rusting
thing, had finally
lurched to a halt,
a death rattle shaking
the frame as the last
drops of oil
sizzled on the hot
roadway. The pickup,
which Mike had nursed
through ten years of
hard, lonely roads,
finally threw a rod
outside Mexican Hat
and it was through
some fluke that he'd
been able to get as far as
the southern edge of
Monument Valley,
almost to the Grand
Canyon exit.

Mike waited for the
USPS Ranger to get
close enough to see him
before he pumped a
couple of rounds of
deer shot into the
radiator, a symbolic
coup-de-gras and flipped
the sawed-off up to
his chin like Lucas
McCain might
have done.

Zoot

I thought I saw the ghost of him
floating over the boulevard
at half past ten last night.
His tenor called to me
down the long corridor of
the Harbor freeway,
distant and haunting
like the final notes from
Micheline's Hohner
lost in the screech of
brakes at ride's end.

I've got it bad.

I thought I felt a strand of
moonbeams or was it
a string of notes, gently
wrapping themselves
around my legs, sending
me tripping across
Hawthorne nights.
Sending me into
a velvet fog so
cool and wet that neither
A Train nor Strayhorn
could guide me
swinging low
back home
to your
lush
life.

And that ain't good.

Love Ends at the Sidewalk

Philosophy not-withstanding
The average does not favor
a reasonable return on your
investment when it comes to
matters of the heart.

As to the force of nature
A man can expect to get
back in spades what he
deserves and then some.

How many shovels does
it take to fill in the hole
left by a lifetime
of bad decisions?

Group Therapy (or One Man's Tasty Morsel...)

I whacked the piñata of
memory until something
flew out and landed on
the floor.

It was gaily wrapped in
colored foil and was quickly
pounced upon by the rest
of the party.

After a brief struggle
someone grabbed it,
tore off the wrapper and
triumphantly held it aloft.

This bright little bauble
from my past was instead
something unnamable,
something dark and shriveled,
something that had long since
lost any real meaning...
and worst of all, something
that looked, for all my best
intentions, like a piece of shit.

Someone tossed it out the window
into the street below where two
dogs got into a fight over which
one of them would get to eat it.

Female Troubles

You can be a nice guy
maybe the nicest guy in the world
But it won't matter, even if
there are extenuating circumstances,
because you are fundamentally
untrustworthy and suspect.
You are a predator, a criminal,
in short, you are a *MAN*.
You are the man behind MANipulator
the man inside MANifesto
MANdate
MANeater
MANeuver
MANgle
MANia
MANnequin
MAN-of-war
MANufacture
MANure
MANslaughter
never mind MANkind
or MANdolin
or even MANhattan

Your inherrent criminal nature
and the ticking clock of instinct
marked you as trouble long ago
You are a liability from whom
justice (a woman coincidently)
expects its due
waiting for it to arrive
express mail (overnight delivery)
sitting by the door
patting the rolling pin lightly
wondering
what your excuse will be this time
ready to drop you like the
sack-of-shit that EVERY woman
knows you are...
she'll be waiting for you
to come tippin' in late
long after curfew's expired

waiting for you like a
Patsy Cline random-driveby
nightmare jukebox

waiting for you like

a just-got-into-town deathrow
hail Mary, long shot

waiting for you like
there is no tomorrow
no past
only today, now

and in that now
you have no history
only herstory and
it's the only story in town
and that story isn't your story
because your story is nothing
but a bold-faced lie!

So go ahead
what will your opening
gambit be?
The clock is ticking.
all eyes are on you
and justice is waiting
like a forgotten anti-personnel
mine, waiting for your
first
innocent
miss-step.

Graduation

"My dad carried
this watch
in his younger
days
and I
carried it
for a while
as a kid."   *(part of a note from my father)*

A simple pocket
watch of no
real value
the kind you
give to a kid
now rests easy
in my pocket
tucked in amid
the keys and
loose change.

Kid that I must be
I love the rituals
of this watch:
it must be wound
every so often
giving one a sense
of time's passage
and yet it has
freed me from
time's yoke thus
releasing me
from time as a
nervous habit.

I'm nearly 50
and I'm more
kid than man
and now I've
got my watch
to prove it's
not gonna get
any better any
time soon.

Next week I'm
gonna check out
becoming a full
blown baby
and start looking
for some Depends.

CORAZON

The walking stick,
leaning in the corner, knows it.
And, so do I: the wanderlust
beckons.

Soon enough -
you're silhouette in the doorway,
slipping my embrace,
the long shadow,
the creaking of the gate,
the final wave from the crest
of the hill.

The wind that whistles
through the treetops
will bring nothing
but the memory
of your sighs.
Though I search the sky
for a message, I will
find only clouds,
feathers and dust,
pale light and a hint of winter
(no trace of you).
Now it begins
this season of long shadows
and the silence of stone.

Coming of Age

It seems like only a few years ago
that I found myself annoyed with
older people, principally my parents
and their friends, who would spend
the bulk of the conversation talking
about the different medications that
they were taking for their various
illnesses and aches and pains.
Now, as I stand in Aisle 15 and
survey the array of "do-it-yourself"
remedies, I wish I had paid better
attention... or taken notes.

You Can't Car-jack A Poem

"I coulda bought a Lexus for that..." poet referring to the cost of his MFA

The MFA diploma suggests that
you CAN write your way out
of a paper bag or at least teach
someone else "how to"
It does not suggest that you
have the brains to get yourself
out of awkward situations that
sometimes arise in the urban
jungle: muggings or home-
invasion robberies or car-theft.
The poet bemoans the lost
revenues that could have been spent
more-or-less wisely on cheap thrills
instead of the investment in one's
future job security -- a symbolized
in a handsome leather-bound tome:
The Collected Works of...
But the chances are slim that you
will be killed over The Collected Works
unless you tried to use said Works
as a shield to stop the reign of lead...

So be proud of your craft Mr. Poet,
though editors may run "chop shops"
under the guise of magazines,
and there may be little riches to be had
in the 'setting down of the lines, the good words'
be safe in the knowledge that no one
wants your Work so bad that they
would kill you for it
(at least,
not yet).

Broken

On Christmas day
I glimpsed my depravity
and set a trap to capture it.
For bait I set out my lost
innocence and waited for
my depravity to come sniffing
around. I didn't have to
wait long. But I was
surprised at how aged and
tired it seemed to be. I had
no difficulty capturing the sorry
old beast in a cage that I
constructed out of miss-begotten
plans and ideas (whose time
had long since gone).

My depravity was just
a ghost of its former self --
once vibrant and alive, now
it had become old and tired
and kind of raggedy --
not much of a force to be
reckoned with. Yet it was
Christmas day and I thought
that I should at least play
with this 'toy'.

But, like an obsession that
one thinks they must have,
I came to see that my "new"
plaything was not what I expected
it to be and I was tired of it
before the day was over.
It was *not* that thing that
had stirred me to action
with its flaming, pulsing
electric shimmerations.
It was no longer a sparkler
grunting in the dark night of
the soul. It was a faded trinket
from an outdated nightmare, a
dream from simpler times,
threadbare and wornout,
no longer a wild thing
to be feared and hunted.

My depravity was a sorry
old beast, ready for the glue
factory. I hated it for what
it had become. It stank of
age and misuse. I put a bullet
into it and listened to it howl.

At last it had some life.

When I was 17

I always think of my father
whenever I hear this old
Frank Sinatra/Nelson Riddle classic

The song isn't completely accurate
as a timeline paralleling his life
but the feeling that it evokes,
the feeling of nostalgic satisfaction
of a life well/miss spent
a not too insulting smugness
the idea that one could
have a "very good year"
that one's memories could
be a "vintage wine"
that Frank and all his swingin' cats
could come to symbolize the best
that this century had to offer

What must he think of as he squints
into the past, searching the horizon,
looking back through the hazy
shadows of memory
tracing the journey from 1928
to 1999, his seventy one years
flipping past like calendar pages
in an old-time movie

The final chorus is coming
the orchestra is welling up
a glass of wine filled to the brim
the last line of the song
is the same as the first
a biblical paraphrasing
It's time to cue the strings
Get ready for that final, sharp note

When I was 17

Lucid Thought #3

Today, while I was cutting
in the stucco trim with a
second coat of enamel
I had a great idea for a
poem. But since I was
up on a ladder and with
nothing to take notes on
(hey, it wasn't *my* wall)
I was forced to try and
remember it <u>later</u>... This
is me trying to remember
it later... without much
luck. And I'm struggling
now to pull that fragment
out of the swirling mess
that is my brain and all
I get is the fact that you
are twenty-one hours away
from me and one of the stars
in the constellation called
the Big Dipper is actually
a galaxy and something
about how the full moon
on the winter solstice this
year will be the closest to
the earth in years and will
exert an extra amount of
pull on those of us who
are inclined toward *lunacy*
and I realize that the poem
is forming anyway and it's
not going to be that great one
I glimpsed today, but couldn't
capture. Instead, it would be
this one:

Twenty-one hours away
and my head is as clogged
as a broken sewer line, my
ideas are being forced to
back up on each other
blending and losing their
individuality like stars in
a galaxy glimpsed from far away.

Twenty-one hours away
and there is a star missing
from my favorite constellation.
I don't know if it has
anything to do with you

but the romantic in me
would like to think that
it does, so I listen to that
romantic part and wonder
if it might be true...
I mean about the star...

I guess I am the muddled old
motherfucker you always
suspected I was, after all.

White Whine

He was weak
his weakness was sad
pathetic
unrestrained
it seeped out from
under his soles
it dripped from
his cuffs
from his sad
puppy dog eyes.

He was a doormat
a spittoon
spent cartridge
whipped dog
rusty can

cast adrift
in a sea of someone
else's possibilities

and he was weak.

Yet, in his weakness
as I listened to him droning on
I began to see my
own weakness
I began to understand
the isolation of weakness
the utter desolation of image
the erasure of any
concept of "self"
of one's value

until the lowest common
denominator remained
and he was this denominator.

And when, at last, I understood
the power of Weakness
I thanked him
sent him on his way
and reflected on this gift
of insight he had brought to me.

And thanked God that things weren't as bad as they had seemed thirty minutes before he arrived.

Unseasonable Weather

The San Gabriels are crowned
With an odd white powder
Like Old Bob, who's hair turned
Snowy white - over night
The day after the Dodgers
traded Mike Piazza away.

Tweeker Afternoon

Playing Mumbly-Peg with Carmen and Eddie
As fat drops of rain preview the beginning of Spring.
Eddie's knife lands like a sudden rejection
The linoleum floor is a sea of tiny incisions.

Tomb

Alone in a tomb of words
I ply my wares
dispensing the "poetic vision"
from my six foot by seven foot
writing cell, here in this
second floor apartment
with its noisy neighbors
slamming doors late
or early – it's no matter
where life buzzes all
around me like
nervous insects.

The Shade-tree Mechanic

In his younger daze
Spanish Mike spent
many hours draped over
the fender of a fifties
truck of some make or model.
With a fist full of wrenches
and a mouth full of cuss words
Mike tackled everything from
the simple point adjustment
to the major overhaul
unfazed by his lack of
knowledge and fueled
by an insatiable curiosity
his faith in the sanctity
of American know-how
and the knowledge that god
was on *our* side.

Years before that incident
on the outskirts of Mexican Hat
Spanish Mike swore that he
would never touch an engine
that didn't have a GM sticker on it somewhere
or a set of points. That all
changed in the 80s when Mike
discovered that even his beloved Jimmy
looked like a goddamned rice-burner
under the hood, where it really counts.

Last time I saw him, he was
just a shade tree alcoholic,
God-less and broken,
his precious know-how,
nowhere to be found, muttering
something about metrics
and quantum mechanics...

You can't tighten your nuts
when the wrenches don't fit.

Photo by Hank Conn

RD has been laboring in the trenches of the Alternative Small Press since 1996, both as editor/publisher of **The Lummox Journal** and as publisher of the **Little Red Book** series with nearly sixty titles by some of the ASP's best/least known poets. In the Lummox Journal's one hundred and twelve issues, he interviewed nearly one hundred poets, writers and artists, always with the emphasis on their creative process.

Although he has been writing off and on since 1968, his most prolific period began in 1993. Since then he has written poetry, short-fiction and essays. Some of those poems appear in this volume. Three of his long road poems are included in **On/Off the Beaten Path**.

RD Armstrong's books include PEDRO BLUE (Vinegar Hill Press), Paper Heart (Lummox Press), In Memoriam (The Inevitable Press), The San Pedro Poems (Lummox Press), RoadKill (12 Gauge Press), Last Call: the Legacy of Charles Bukowski and The Hunger (both by Lummox Press). His poems have been published in over one hundred small press magazines and on over sixty websites. This year also saw the publication of **Fire & Rain Vols. 1 & 2**, as well as **El Pagano & Other Twisted Tales** (short stories).

Visit **www.lummoxpress.com** for a complete picture of RD's empire.

www.ingramcontent.com/pod-product-compliance
Lightning Source LLC
Chambersburg PA
CBHW071951090426
42740CB00011B/1891